Anonymous

Two Months in Palestine

or, a Guide to a Rapid Journey to Chief Places of Interest in the Holy Land

Anonymous

Two Months in Palestine
or, a Guide to a Rapid Journey to Chief Places of Interest in the Holy Land

ISBN/EAN: 9783348061056

Printed in Europe, USA, Canada, Australia, Japan

Cover: Foto ©Andreas Hilbeck / pixelio.de

More available books at **www.hansebooks.com**

TWO MONTHS IN PALESTINE:

OR,

A Guide to a Rapid Journey

TO

THE CHIEF PLACES OF INTEREST IN THE HOLY LAND.

BY

THE AUTHOR OF "TWO MONTHS IN SPAIN," "THE MERCHANT'S HOLIDAY," ETC.

———————————

LONDON:

NISBET AND CO., 21, BERNERS STREET.

1870.

PREFACE.

THE greater portion of the following chapters appeared in the "Leisure Hour" of last year. Many of the friends of the Author, at home and in India, having expressed an opinion that, if his journal were published with fuller details and directions, to serve as a guide, it might be useful to those who wish to make a short journey to the East, as well as to the general reader, the Author therefore ventures to offer this volume to the public.

Among those to whom the Author hopes his hints may be useful, are the numerous passengers now travelling to and from India and Australia, who may wish to change the old beaten track, direct to Alexandria. They may follow the routes described in the following pages, and at the cost of a very little additional time and money, greatly add to their enjoyment and knowledge.

The homeward-bound passengers coming through the Suez Canal may take boat at Port Said for Jaffa, and visit the chief places of interest in the Holy Land, and re-embark at Beyrout, either for Constantinople or Trieste.

The Author has to acknowledge with many thanks the great kindness and courtesy of the proprietors of the "Leisure Hour" in allowing him the privilege of republishing these papers, in their present form.

LONDON, 1st *July*, 1870.

CONTENTS.

LIST OF ILLUSTRATIONS.

TWO MONTHS IN PALESTINE.

CHAPTER I.

HAVING lately returned from a three months' tour in the East, two months of which were spent in Palestine, I indulge a hope that the result of my experience may be useful and interesting to those who contemplate making a short journey to the "Land of the Bible." I may say at once that I have no intention of exhausting the patience of the reader with lengthened descriptions or reflections. Those who wish to become better acquainted with the history, ancient and modern, of the Holy Land, will find, in volumes more than I can enumerate, from Josephus to the latest productions of Stanley, Robinson, Thomson, Tristram, and other eminent writers, all the information they can desire. My sole aim in this volume is to give a practical detail of the journey, touching slightly on the present state of those sacred places with which our earliest

B

and best associations are interwoven, and pointing out to future travellers, whose time and means may be limited to a rapid journey, the result of my own experience, with such suggestions as may have occurred to me in my pilgrimage.

There are several routes open to travellers proceeding to the East. There is the old and well-known track by Marseilles and Malta, which we will dismiss at once, as all travellers are familiar with it, and all old Indians tired of it. The next is the journey through Italy, and from Brindisi to Alexandria. The next two routes are through North and South Germany, the former by the way of Cologne, Hanover, Berlin, Dresden, Prague, through Bohemia to Vienna, and on by rail to Trieste, for the Austrian Lloyd's steamer. These may be slightly varied according to the time and taste of the traveller. Being already familiar with these three routes, I took new ground by the way of Constantinople, and for the information of the reader will slightly sketch the journey from my starting-point.

I may first premise that my luggage consisted of a convenient sized portmanteau, weighing, with contents, about fifty pounds. On a journey of this kind it is neither desirable nor necessary to take a large wardrobe. I had three flannel shirts and a small assortment of linen and warm under-clothing; and, strapped together, a large Scotch plaid and great coat, a pair of long boots to come over the knees, and a sheet of india-rubber cloth and umbrella completed my luggage. Any mistakes into which I fell with respect to this outfit I shall point out in the progress of my journey.

I would not recommend the traveller to burden himself with too many books. I had several volumes with me that I had scarcely time to look at. Murray's two volumes on "Syria and Palestine" are better adapted for the literary man than for the tourist, for they go into too long and elaborate details. The proper English guide-book for Palestine has yet to be written. "They manage these things better in France." I found ten persons out of twelve that I travelled with armed with a small but sufficient French guide-book. It may be superficial, but it contains in one volume all the information that is necessary on a rapid journey. Murray divides his volumes into "South and North Palestine;" the index is in the second volume, so that we cannot make reference to the first without having the second at hand. If any extra volume is taken, perhaps Dr. Thomson's "Land and the Book" is us

good as any.   I conclude that every pilgrim travels
with his Bible, which, apart from higher obligations, is the one essential guide to the Holy Land.

With regard to the expenses, I may say at once
that no experience of European travelling is any
guide to the calls on the pocket in Palestine.   One
will be safe to calculate the expense of the journey
at £2 a day, or say £180 for three months.   I had
circular notes to that amount from the Union Bank
of London, and only brought back £20, with the
most economical management.

I had an old passport with me, and was only twice
called upon during my journey to produce it.   The
first time was at Rustchuk, on the Danube, where
the Greek *employé* kept it for a few minutes, and
brought it back without any *visé*, but with a demand
for four piasters, of which I took no notice.   The next
call was on landing at Jaffa; but this was a mere
claim for "backsheesh," and I gave the needy sup-
plicant two piasters to get rid of his importunity.

Thus lightly equipped, I started from London on
the evening of the 8th of October, with a through
ticket, by mixed train, "London to Munich, £5 11s."
This entitled me to first-class as far as Cologne, and
from thence second-class. Most travellers will prefer
the latter, as the carriages are the same, and one has

a chance of more intelligent, or at least more communicative, companions. I arrived at Brussels at 7
A.M., and at Cologne at 4 P.M., where we remained
two hours, allowing time for dinner and to visit our
interminable old friend, the Cathedral, which is " to
be finished in eight years " from any given time. I
took the next train for Coblentz, where I remained
for the night, and next day had an opportunity of
seeing the most beautiful and picturesque scenery of
the Rhine. Though railway speed is not the best
mode of seeing the landscape to advantage, it is
pleasant to look over this romantic stream on those
picturesque hills that rise from the right bank of
the river, with villages, ruined castles, and richly
cultivated vineyards opening out to the sight, as the
train rounds the spurs of the left bank, or emerges
from the cuttings.

At Mayence we crossed the river, and went on
to Darmstadt and Aschaffenburg. Here we entered
Bavaria, and proceeded along the valley of the
Maine. This is amongst the finest railway journeys
in Europe. The beautiful hills rise on each side of
the valley, clothed with pine, birch, and oak, now in
rich autumn tints. The broad, clear stream, winding
through forests and green meadows, reminded me of
the scenery in the valley of the Tay from Dunkeld

to Taymouth. At Wurzburg we changed carriages
for Munich, the direct train going on to Ratisbon
and Passau for Vienna, and the Munich line striking
south by Augsburg. At 10 P.M. the second day from
London we arrived at Munich, where I remained
two days to see the rich treasures of art of which this
city boasts. I had not been in this city before, and
took the opportunity to visit its celebrated galleries
of paintings and sculpture, which are only second
to those of Florence; and to inspect the extensive
bronze works, in which are to be seen the casts of
statuary sent to all parts of the world; and the
celebrated glass-painting establishments, so well
known for their beautiful colouring and designs.
These were all open to visitors at this time, and
I felt amply rewarded for these two days' delay.

I left at 7 A.M. for Vienna, thirteen hours by railway, passing Salzburg and Lintz. I had a strong
hankering to remain a day at Salzburg. The peep
caught from the station made a vivid impression on
my mind, which was afterwards confirmed by reading the late Sir David Wilkie's faithful description of
the situation:—" It is Edinburgh Castle and the Old
Town brought within the cliffs of the Trossachs, and
watered by the river Tay." After a delightful day's
journey, I arrived at Vienna at 10 P.M. There I

remained three days, renewing my acquaintance with this ever-attractive capital, and to take a note of the great improvements that are going forward both materially and politically. It is not my intention to describe the many attractions of this city. Suffice it to say that, in palatial architecture, in the broad avenues, gardens, promenades with flowers and shrubbery, fountains and statuary, which now cover the site of the old moat and glacis that surrounded the old city, it almost rivals the Paris of Haussmann.

No traveller could well pass through Vienna without making some stay. Three or four days may suffice for a hasty visit to the chief objects of interest. First among these should be the Upper and Lower Belvedere, with their galleries of art and antiquity, including a magnificent collection of paintings, consisting of nearly 2,000 works, all admirably arranged under the different schools and carefully catalogued. Next in importance is the Imperial Palace, with its museum, cabinet of gems, and antiquities. The cathedral church of St. Stephen's, which is still undergoing repair, is among the finest specimens of lofty and elaborate Gothic architecture that we have in Europe. The burial vaults of the imperial family, in the Capuchin church, are also worthy of a visit, from their great historical interest.

An intelligent guide, who speaks French or English, may be engaged at the hotel at three flórins (6s.) a day, and it is as well to arrange with him, before starting, what places can be visited and what charges are to be made in the shape of douceur, etc. The day's enjoyment may be wound up by a drive round the circle or boulevards, and through the Prater, the Hyde Park of Vienna; and, to the healthy traveller, the unrivalled *cuisine* of the " Hotel Archduke Charles" will compensate for any fatigue of body or mind.

CHAPTER II.

On the 16th of October I started for Pesth by railway. The distance is 171 miles, and occupies about eight hours. A few miles beyond Vienna the railway skirts the memorable battle-field of Wagram; but there are few objects of interest on this line. No one in search of the picturesque need take this journey—all is flat, tame, and monotonous; but the wide plains of wheat and maize-growing lands would gladden the heart of a Midlothian or Ayrshire farmer.

We cannot help observing great neglect, indolence, and apparent poverty among the peasantry. But when we consider what this country has suffered; how long it was the battle-field of Turk and Christian; and, in later years, its struggles and sufferings under the military tyranny and heavy taxation of its Austrian rulers, it is not to be wondered at that a state of discontent, neglect, and indifference may still be traced along these half-cultivated plains. It is, however, very satisfactory to know that this state of things is rapidly changing for the better.

The scenery and appearance of the country improve as we approach Pesth. The spurs of the southern Alps close round the Danube, and are richly clothed with vines, and wooded to their summit.

I had been recommended to the "Hotel Frohuer," and had nothing particular to complain of, except that its great feature was a large noisy billiard-room, to which every other arrangement was subservient.

I had the good fortune to have an introduction to the Rev. Mr. König, of the Jewish Mission, from whom I received great attention and much information. This has been one of the most successful missions among the Jews. There are about two million Protestants in Hungary, but they do not appear to be increasing. There seems to have been a long epoch of sceptical indifference amongst the people in matters of religion, which has been only within the last few years broken by missionary influence, commencing at the time when Dr. Keith and others visited Hungary and the East as a deputation from the Church of Scotland.

I may mention here that the Protestant Mission

Schools are not confined to any particular sect, but number about 400 children of various religions. All read the Old and New Testament without any scruples, and, whatever may be the effect of home influence, there can be no doubt that the knowledge thus acquired must in time produce its fruits.

One cannot pass through Hungary without feeling great interest in its past history and in its future progress. Like Poland and Italy, and other "oppressed nationalities," it has commanded a large amount of English sympathy. To me it has a still further interest, as I find a strong analogy in many respects between this people and the Highlanders of Scotland. The reader of history will remember that some time in the ninth century a hardy and warlike gang of a mixed Turco race crossed the Carpathian mountains, and in a few years conquered the whole of the country now called Hungary and became its feudal lords. These Magyars were a restless, brave, and warlike people, who held the profession of arms in the highest esteem, and looked on trade and commerce as altogether below their dignity, and exercised much the same authority over their vassals as did our Highland chieftains.

Probably about the same period of history some hordes of Scandinavian pirates and robbers crossed

the northern seas, and took possession of the islands
and highlands of Scotland, built castles and strong-
holds along the coast, and subjected the native Celts
to their authority. The successors of these Norse-
men, wrapping a piece of checkered cloth around
the lower part of their body, and sticking a feather
in their cap, called themselves "Highland Chieftains;" and to this day the difference of race is so
perceptible that any stranger travelling in the highlands of Scotland will at once observe the marked
difference between the tall, fair-complexioned
Scandinavian type, and the short, dark Celt. I
have drawn this parallel between these two nations
to account for the warlike spirit of their leaders.
Our countrymen of the north have long learned the
advantages of peace and commerce. Hungary is
now, I hope, on the road to the same happy results,
when the Magyars shall be as loyal, peaceful, and
industrious subjects under a united government as
our Scottish Highlanders are now to Great Britain.

Curiously enough, the men who were formerly the
most patriotic and national are now the chief
obstacles to union and progress. They may be right
or wrong in their opposition to centralisation, and
the introduction of the German element into the
government ; but it is to be feared that this antago-

nism may retard the political and social progress of the nation.

There is still a strong tinge of Orientalism in the character and manners of the Magyars, an inclination to indolence and selfish enjoyments, and indifference to changes and improvements. The most active and industrious men that we see in Buda-Pesth and other large towns seem to be the Germans, of whom the Jews form a considerable number.

During my stay at Pesth I called on my old friend General Klapka, whom I knew in London in the days of his exile. I was introduced by him to the Diet, or House of Assembly. The discussions were very free and very animated, a sort of compound between the British Parliament and American Congress. The comforts and convenience of the House are very much superior to our Houses of Parliament, notwithstanding the millions we have paid for architecture and decoration. The two cities of Pesth and Buda are connected by a magnificent suspension bridge, constructed by an Englishman. The view from the old palace on the heights of Buda, over the Danube and city, is grand and imposing. The situation is admirably adapted for trade. Since the reconciliation with Austria the inhabitants have

increased 30,000, and mills and manufactories are
springing up all along the banks of the river.

I left Pesth at 10 P.M. on the 20th, by railway,
paying £10 for rail and boat to Constantinople, including food, and arrived at Baziasch, on the
Danube, at 10 A.M. next morning. The boat which
should have been awaiting us did not arrive, in
consequence of the low state of the river, till 5 P.M.,
when we went on board and dined, and lay to during
the night. Before daylight we were transferred to
a smaller boat, in which we proceeded as far as the
rapids, or the iron gates of the Danube.

As we descend the river the scenery improves,
and nearing Orsova, where the spurs of the Carpathian range of mountains approach, and appear to
block the passage of the river, ·the scenery is magnificent, and the impression left on my mind was that
I had never seen anything grander or more picturesque on any river in Europe. These mountain
spurs are richly clothed with trees and shrubs, now
in all their beautiful autumnal tints. Now we approach a gorge where the mountains rise abruptly
from the banks of the river, as if they had been cleft
asunder by an earthquake, and now we see them
rising in gentle wooded slopes. Every reach brought
a fresh view, so varied and picturesque that the eye

and the mind never flagged. The river was too low at this season to sail entirely through the rapids, and we had to disembark, and for a few miles were conveyed in some very rickety old traps for a little distance below the falls, and past the old island fort, where we joined a larger boat. I was not sorry for this change of transit, as it gave us a chance of seeing something of the character and habitations of the Wallachian peasantry. I had heard of the degraded state of these Danubian provinces, but was not prepared for the sight of such squalor and apparent misery. The villages were mere pigsties, in which men and animals wallowed, scarcely to be distinguished from each other. The men and boys were clothed in sheepskin jackets with the wool outside, and little else, and certainly presented a most savage appearance.

We again re-embarked and lay to for the night; and all next day were sailing on the broad stream of the Danube; and at 5 P.M. reached Rustchuk. This is the river terminus of the Varna railway, and here we landed and slept for the night, as the train did not leave till the following morning.

We left by train at 7 A.M. The distance from Rustchuk to Varna is 140 miles, and occupies about ten hours. There seems to be very little traffic, and although we stopped at a number of small stations, no passengers or goods joined or left us. Unless the shareholders, who are chiefly English, have some better guarantee for their dividends than the profits of the traffic, I doubt if the line can pay. Turkey is not yet sufficiently· advanced for railways, and if my advice were asked, with regard to investing in them, it would be that given by *Punch* to parties about to marry—" Don't."

The journey was a very pleasant one through Bulgaria. The railway makes an ascent of 2,000 feet through varied and picturesque scenery; but again, it was painful to witness the ragged, dirty, and degraded state of the peasantry. The inhabitants of these provinces seem to combine.the worst elements of the Christians and Turks without any of their virtues.

We reached Varna before sunset, skirting those dreary plains so bitterly remembered by those who survived the trials and sufferings of our fine army before it embarked for the Crimea. There is no harbour at Varna, and, as the steamers lie some distance off, we were taken on board in small boats. Fortunately the weather was fine, otherwise it must be both uncomfortable and dangerous going out to vessels riding in the Black Sea.

We found a large and comfortable steamer, of the Austrian Lloyd's Company, waiting for us, and shortly after we embarked we were called down to a most sumptuous and *recherché* dinner. The dining-saloon was well filled with a cheerful and agreeable company. We soon got under way. The sea was as calm as a mill-pond, lighted up by a beautiful clear moon, and we were able to walk the deck and enjoy our cigar and conversation to a late hour.

A little after sunrise next morning we entered the far-famed Bosphorus. This passage is worthy of all the praise that poets and painters have bestowed upon it. A beautiful sheet of water, from two to three miles broad, and about twenty miles between the two seas. The hills of Europe and Asia rise on each side, covered with verdure, and along the margin of the dark, deep waters are studded the palaces and gardens of the Sultan, and the mansions of the wealthy pashas and merchants of Constantinople. As we approach the city the scene is beyond all description. The Seraglio Point, the Golden Horn, Galata, and Pera rising over the hill to the right, and to the left Scutari, with Florence Nightingale's hospital, and the sad memorial of the ten thousand brave men, the victims of war and disease, whose bodies now lie mouldering

c

on the heights that overlook the Sea of Marmora, all these are familiar by name to most of us; but no pen or pencil can do justice to the sight. Yet nothing can be more deplorable than the interior of this beautiful picture. And every day we remained only added to our grief at the thought of such a region being in the hands of a people and a government without vitality, and without a single element of progress.

On the steamer coming to anchor we were soon surrounded with boats, and such a Babel of languages, such fighting, tearing, and swearing, between Maltese, Levantine, Greek, and Arab boatmen, that we were glad to put ourselves in the hands of an attendant from the "Hôtel Angleterre." On landing we were not called upon to go to the Custom House. Our baggage was light, and we were passed by the Custom House officer, on the payment of a few piasters, without the trouble of opening our portmanteau. A hamal, or porter, was engaged to carry our packages; and mounting ponies, we followed our guide through the winding, dirty, crowded streets of Galata, to the hospitable hotel of Mr. Missiri, on the heights of Pera.

CHAPTER III.

THE manner in which I spent my week may be briefly referred to for the guidance of tourists whose time may be limited. The first excursion should be a sail across to Scutari, looking in on the "Howling Dervishes," and passing on to the great barracks, once the British hospital, immortalised by the noble labours of Florence Nightingale and her companions. A little beyond this is the English burial-ground, to which we are guided by the prominent, and what is called "ugly memorial," by the late Baron Marochetti. Here an hour may be passed in sorrowful contemplation among the graves and mementoes of the dead. One day will suffice for old Stamboul. The Seraglio, so well known through poets and painters, was burned down in 1866, and all that portion that skirted the sea is being cleared away. From the gardens of the old palace the hill rises in gentle undulations, and crowning one of these heights is the celebrated mosque of St. Sophia, the earliest and best specimen we have of Byzantine architecture;

but, like all things Turkish, whether religious or secular, showing marks of neglect and decay. We had a special order to visit this mosque, which, with guide, cost us ten francs each. There is little left of the rich and beautiful details of the Church of Justinian, the description of which now reads like a romance, except it may be those ancient columns of marble, porphyry, and granite, brought from Ephesus, Baalbec, and other early Greek temples.

A glance at the accompanying engraving, from a photograph, will serve better than any description to show the style of the building.

The Mosque of Ahmediah is another fine specimen of architecture, and is cleaner and better kept than St. Sophia, and perhaps more attractive to the superficial observer, being a happy combination of the Greek and Saracenic styles, and very imposing in its appearance. I may just refer to one other mosque, which should not be overlooked, viz., that of Suleiman, on a wing of which is the splendid tomb of Sultan Soliman. Among the objects of great interest in this neighbourhood are the remains of the Roman aqueduct and great cistern of "a thousand columns." The arched roof of this great area is supported by nearly 300 columns, of fifty to sixty feet from their base, and forming a complete labyrinth

INTERIOR OF THE MOSQUE OF ST. SOPHIA.

of passages, which are now occupied by silk-winders
and rope-spinners. The bazaars are objects of great
attraction to those who have never seen any Oriental
city, and are perhaps as good specimens of indolence,
dirt, and confusion, as can be seen anywhere from
Constantinople to Cabul. On our second visit to the
old city we ascended the Venetian, or what is called
the "Genoese" tower, which stands on one of
the "seven hills," and whence there is a panoramic
view unequalled in the world, embracing the Sea of
Marmora, the Golden Horn, and the Bosphorus, and
from the old walls and towers on the north to the
heights of Scutari and the distant mountains of Asia
on the south, with all the intermediate buildings,
rising terrace above terrace, with towers, cupolas,
and minarets lighted up with a bright sun and clear
blue sky. From this tower we rode out by what are
called the "seven towers," and the old wall of
Theodosius, and round to the upper end of the
Golden Horn, where we dismissed our ponies, and
sailed down the Horn, passing the arsenal and small
fleet of ironclads, on which the Sultan has lavished
large sums of borrowed money to very little purpose.

Nothing can be more delightful than sailing along
these waters; and as it was my privilege to have
introductions to our missionaries residing on the

borders of the Golden Horn and the Bosphorus, some of the pleasantest days of my sojourn were spent in visiting their schools, and in their society. This is scarcely the place to speak of the labours and Christian devotion of these good men and women. I shall have occasion more than once to refer to our Protestant missions in the East, and I can never do so but with feelings of gratitude and of admiration, not only for their Christian teaching, but for their civilising example to the nominal Christians and the heathen around them. I have often felt pained and surprised to hear some of our countrymen attempting to throw ridicule on these efforts to spread the light of the gospel and a better education among the heathen, and questioning the influence of these missions. I only wish that these sceptics could see the devoted and self-denying lives of these men, and then, perhaps, their charity would not "begin (*and end*) at home." There is no city in the world in which there is such scope and necessity for Protestant missionary labour as in this capital of the Turkish empire. Such a variety of religions and nationalities are found in antagonism, rivalling each other in ignorance and superstition; and with some of these so-called Christians even the Turk, bad as he is, may be favourably contrasted.

Before quitting Constantinople, I may mention that the traveller will find it a very expensive place. The three or four hotels in Pera charge from sixteen to twenty francs a day, exclusive of wine. Missiri's, "Hôtel Angleterre," where I took up my quarters, is as good as any. The landlord, who was a dragoman, and travelled with the author of "Eothen," is a very useful and intelligent man, and Mrs. Missiri, who is an English-woman, understands and attends carefully to the comforts of her English guests. The expenses for guides, horses, boats, and backsheesh of all kinds will not be short of sixteen francs more, so that, if one moves about daily, a week's expense will not be much short of £12.

On arranging to proceed on my journey, I found that the Austrian Lloyd's, French, and Russian boats, all sailed for Alexandria, calling only at Smyrna, and the following week calling at Joppa and other Syrian ports. I had, therefore, no alternative but to wait another week at Constantinople, or proceed as far as Smyrna, and remain there till the boats of the following week passed on their voyage to Beyrout and Jaffa, which I did.

On the 30th October we embarked on the Austrian Lloyd's steamer for Smyrna, and sailed at

4 P.M. The weather was delightful, and as we moved slowly round the Seraglio Point into the Sea of Marmora the scene was magnificent. The setting sun was bathing in golden tints the domes and minarets of the city, and the surrounding hills, and all would have been like a fairy landscape but for the crowd and confusion on board. There were upwards of 200 deck passengers, consisting of Turks, Jews, Greeks, and Armenians, most of the first on their pilgrimage to Mecca, a motley, noisy, quarrelsome group. There were great complaints among the first-class passengers, who had paid a very high rate for the comforts of the quarter-deck, and found they had not a foot of space to walk upon. Half the poop deck was railed off for the women, and the remainder, as well as the quarter-deck, was covered with mats, mattresses, and quilts, about which the men were quarrelling and coming to blows. The fire from matches, pipes, and cheroots, was flying about in all directions, enough to create alarm in timid minds; but those whose duty it was to attend to these matters seemed to take things very coolly. The Turks were about the best behaved of the lot, and if I had not been somewhat accustomed to Oriental life and habits, I should have expected

nothing short of mutiny and bloodshed. By 10 P.M.
we had all shaken down pretty comfortably into
our places. I found I had my berth in a cabin
with the Bishop of Gibraltar. I had witnessed his
consecration of the "Memorial" Church at Constantinople, and had attended the service conducted
by him on the first Sunday after, and though it
was a little too ritualistic for my taste, I had no
reason to complain of his social intercourse, and
found his lordship a most courteous and pleasant
cabin companion.

Soon after daylight the following morning we
entered the Dardanelles, having previously stopped
two hours at Gallipoli, which will always be associated with the names of those gallant men who
fell victims to that short but sad episode in our
history, the Crimean war. Soon after entering the
straits between the castles and batteries lying on
each side, we anchored at Abydos. We talked
over the romantic feat of Leander. About noon
we passed the mouth of the river Meander, and discussed the supposed site of ancient Troy, the very
existence of which, it seems, is denied in these
sceptical days. At dusk we anchored off Mitylene,
a city interesting to the Christian, being identified
with St. Paul and the other apostles. The town,

rising up from the bay, and the hills around it, a
bright moon lighting up their summits, reminded
,me of Rothesay; but in no other respect does it
resemble that quiet and eminently Christian town,
for even our Greek and Turkish passengers pronounced it to be "the most unsafe and wicked
place in all Asia Minor." Early next day we arrived at Smyrna. There are two good hotels here,
viz., the Deux Augustes, and the Hôtel de l'Europe.
These rival hotels were each anxious to catch a
bishop, and as I had a long white beard, which the
good bishop had not, and was dressed in black,
with a broad-brimmed felt hat turned up at the
sides, the touters that came on shore with me made
sure that they had secured the sacred treasure, and
left the worthy bishop behind to be conveyed to
the Hôtel de l'Europe. I was ushered into my
apartments with great ceremony, and I soon after
descended to lunch; there were several gentlemen
at the table, who rose and received me with marked
respect. A little conversation soon dispelled the
illusion, which was followed by a roar of laughter
at the disappointment of the Deux Augustes. The
Egyptian boat left for the Syrian coast the morning I arrived, and I was very much disappointed
at having to remain here for a week, but can now

look back with great pleasure to the social intercourse and information, and small excursions, which
I enjoyed during that time. Some of the gentlemen
at the hotel were connected with the railway from
Smyrna to Aidin, and were well acquainted with
this district. They spoke with enthusiasm of the
vast resources of the country, both vegetable and
mineral, which, under any other government but
that of Turkey, would be one of the richest in the
world. It was here that I first heard the phrase,
or rather the curse against an enemy, " May Allah
send you Sheikhs!" and no one can understand
the force of this bitter infliction till they have
travelled in the East, and seen and heard of the
corruption and injustice of these greedy and selfish
men.

   In describing the resources and capabilities of
the country, engineers and mineralogists, missionaries and merchants, all are agreed that it is the
richest and most neglected of the possessions of
Turkey, and that from Armenia to the Ægean
coast, and from the Black Sea to the Mediterranean,
there is no finer country on the globe,—with the exception, perhaps, of the peninsula of Spain and
Portugal, which it very much resembles; but all
of them had the same sad tale of stagnation, neg-

lect, and oppression. They speak of the Sultan as "indulging in freaks of purchasing iron-clad ships, and building palaces, but being totally indifferent to the progress and happiness of his people;" and that the sort of liberty which his subjects and aliens now enjoy, is entirely of a negative character, arising partly from indifference, and partly out of compliment to the support which he receives from Western Europe; but even the liberties conceded to his own subjects are a dead letter when left to be carried out by corrupt officials. For example, the law is, that the evidence of a Christian should be taken for its full value, against a Mohammedan; but it is not so in any court beyond the reach of our consuls. Again, a Christian woman leaving her husband, and becoming a Mohammedan, the husband is entitled to claim the children; but this law is frequently violated, and the husband would endanger his life by attempting to assert his right, unless he were rich enough to buy over the officers of—injustice.

In our short journeys as far as Aiden we saw extensive tracts of country, capable of the highest cultivation, lying neglected and overrun with weeds; and were told that there was no encouragement or safety in extending cultivation. The proprietors were often government officials and collectors of revenue. The peasants were generally indebted to these proprietors, who put the screw on to the last turn, till the energies of the cultivator were paralysed, and any attempt to better his condition or improve the property only resulted in another turn of the screw. These men have bought their office, and they enter on their functions with only one aim and intention, viz., to make it profitable to themselves. Sometimes the crimes and extortions of these officials are represented to head-quarters by persons of some influence, when their ill-gotten gain is confiscated to the State—not for the benefit of the injured and oppressed, but often quite otherwise. The end of this state of affairs cannot be far distant. The so-called progress which politicians and speculators believe to be moving in the Turkish empire is a mere delusion. When the Turk ceased to be a conqueror, he sank down into corruption and decay. In proof of this, almost the whole of their trade is in the hands of Greeks, Armenians, Jews, and a few merchants of Western Europe. The Greeks are a match for all the others; they have few scruples in their ambition to get rich, and are making their way in every mart in the East, even to the capital of British India. Many travellers in the East say they prefer the Turk or Arab to the

Greek in their private dealings. I cannot agree
with this opinion. The commercial morality of the
Greeks, like their Christianity, may be sadly corrupted; but there is a vitality in this small nation
totally beyond the reach of the Turk, which time and
intercourse with the western world will improve.

The line of railway by which I have been travelling from Smyrna to Aidin is the second great line
formed under the auspices of the Turkish Government, with English capital, and seems in a worse
financial condition than the one from Rustchuk to
Varna, to which I referred in a former chapter.
Here there seems to be little or no traffic, either in
passengers or goods. It is a melancholy sight to see
these empty trains, "like a wounded snake dragging
their slow length along," scarcely paying, I should
think, for the coal and grease of the engine. I
believe the shareholders have some sort of guarantee,
into which, as I am not a shareholder, it was not
my business to inquire.

There are few objects now of sacred or classical
interest in Smyrna, but the biblical reader will remember that here was planted one of the "seven
churches of Asia" (Rev. ii. 8). The old castle is
called Genoese, but from the Cyclopean character of
some parts of the ruins, must be of a much earlier

date. It stands at an elevation of 500 feet, overlooking the bay and city and surrounding country,
and is the best point to obtain a good view of the
place. We were provided with donkeys for the
ascent, and had no fatigue, and nothing could surpass the beauty of the scenery around.

I had brought introductions from Constantinople
to some of the missionaries here, to whom, as usual,
I was indebted for information and hospitality.
Among the most noteworthy of the schools is that
of the Deaconesses, conducted by Protestant ladies
from North Germany, assisted by tutors, teachers,
and governesses of other nations. I have never seen
in Europe a better conducted establishment, and one
can scarcely realise the fact of such an oasis of progress and education in the midst of this desert of
ignorance and superstition. Everything about it,
from the white muslin caps of the sisters to the
school-rooms and dormitories of the children, looked
clean and healthy. Within the marble-paved cor-
ridors was a well-cultivated garden, with orange,
lemon, and pomegranate trees, with oleanders and
other flowering shrubs from tropical and temperate
zones. The children were of all nations and religions, Jews, Arabs, Greeks, Latins, and Armenians,
and the range of education is something that would

startle the pretensions of some of our genteel boarding-schools. The Old and New Testaments are class-books; the children are also taught to sing in concert those soft and plaintive German hymns, which one cannot listen to without moisture in his eyes. This institution is now self-sustaining, and has about 200 pupils, from all grades of society; and about forty children in their Orphanage, educated as Protestants.

I cannot say much about the position and progress of the American, English, and Scottish mission schools here. It had been a very unhealthy and unfavourable season, which was assigned me as the reason for the paucity of attendance at their schools. The Scriptures are read also in these schools, which is very properly a *sine qua non* with our missionaries, to which the parents make no objection.

The reader will understand that the missionary who labours amongst the heathen and semi-barbarous people must perform the double functions of school-master and clergyman, and that this is no argument against the advocates of secular instruction amongst our own youth. We have come to the conviction that a certain amount of secular instruction is necessary and due to every child of the nation, apart altogether from religious instruction, which should

D

form a separate duty, and devolve, on parents, priests, and guardians. In the case of these Orientals the advantages of a superior education overcome the scruples of parents, and they hope to counteract the effects of this religious teaching by the influence of home and family ties.

There is no place in Asia Minor more attractive to the Christian pilgrim than Ephesus. Through the kindness of Mr. Cumberbatch, British consul, I got an introduction to Mr. Wood, who is now engaged, for the British Museum, in excavations among the ruins of this city. We made arrangements to start at 4 A.M. by a " goods train," in the guard's van, and in three hours arrived at Ayaslook, the station of Ephesus. My companion told me that the two names mean the same thing, viz., " the city of the moon." We had six or seven hours before us to ramble over the ruins. The weather was superb, with a clear sky and gentle cooling breeze. The ancient city is hidden from the station by the abrupt hill on which it partly stands. We found horses on hire at the station, and no goat could have climbed up and along the face of these hills, and amongst the *débris* of ruins, with more safety than these animals; but for the example of our guide, who seemed to have no value for his neck, I should often have been inclined to dismount, and lead my pony over the ruins and along the terraced vaults in the face of the hill.

Wandering among these ruins, our thoughts turn naturally to the "Acts of the Apostles." The conduct of Demetrius and his craftsmen is so graphically portrayed that one might apply the description to any city within our own time where corporate and "vested interests" were at stake. I must not occupy the reader too long with details, and shall only glance at the present condition of this ancient Greek and early Christian city. Proceeding from the railway-station, at less than a mile distant, we rounded the spur of a hill called "Mount Pion." The first object that attracts attention is the ruins of the Magnesian gate, near to which Mr. Wood has discovered a long colonnade leading to a succession of tombs and sarcophagi, and amongst them the supposed tomb of St. Mark. By this passage he hopes to arrive at the long-disputed site of the great temple of Diana. Proceeding onward, we come to the lately excavated ruins of the Odeon, a small theatre constructed during the best period of Greek art. And farther on, rising over the slope of the hill, and overlooking all other objects, are the ruins of the great theatre.

Nothing but the continued destruction by earth-quakes could have committed such havoc as we see here; no time or human hands could have so shattered and scattered this magnificent edifice. The semicircle, or place of audience, which was said to contain 60,000 people, is cut in the face of the hill, and rises to the height of eighty feet, the out-line of which is still very distinct; the rows of marble seats, now covered with weeds and rubbish, can easily be traced. Looking down from this height on the proscenium, I took the opportunity of reading the 19th chapter of "The Acts," and could see, in my mind's eye, those 60,000 riotous citizens, crowding these benches, hoarse with the cry of "Great is Diana of the Ephesians." "Some there-fore cried one thing, and some another : for the assembly was confused; and the more part knew not wherefore they were come together." Con-siderable excavations have been made round the great proscenium, exhibiting blocks of fine white marble of fifteen to twenty tons weight, their faces carved with festoons and figures, as sharp and beautiful as when they came from the hands of the artists. The same may be said of the other great ruins, the Market, Forum, Gymnasium, Stadium, etc.

There is something sad and solemn mingled with

intense interest and excitement in ruminating among
these ruins. We picture to ourselves this magnificent Græco-Roman city, with probably a quarter of
a million of inhabitants; the great Temple of Diana
—its theatre, gymnasiums, forums, and great port,
connecting the bay with the city; one of the largest
naval and commercial harbours of the Greeks, and
the rival of Athens. We recall the important place
it occupied in sacred history, as one of the Seven
Churches associated with the planting of Christianity. St. Paul, Aquila, Priscilla, St. John, and
St. Timothy, have made the name of Ephesus
familiar to every reader of the sacred volume.

For more than three centuries it remained an unquestioned tradition among the early Christians that
the Virgin Mary accompanied St. John to this city,
and that here she died and was buried. Certainly this
tradition is far more reasonable and probable than
the story told by the Greek and Latin priests in the
so-called "Church and Tomb of the Virgin," outside
the walls of Jerusalem. The bitter hatred and
vindictive persecution of the followers of Christ,
by the Jews, would naturally drive the family
from that condemned city to a place of greater
safety; and what so likely as that the mother of our
Lord should escape under the care of "the beloved

disciple," and seek shelter in Ephesus, where there seems to have been a certain amount of liberty and protection? This we may infer from the words of the chief officer of the city, called in the "Acts" the "town clerk," for when he calmed and reproved the populace, in the chapter to which I have already referred, he told them that "these men are neither robbers of churches, nor blasphemers of your goddess, wherefore if the craftsmen have matter against any man, the law is open, and there are deputies; let them implead one another," etc. From which it is evident that a much greater amount of protection was afforded to the new sect here than in a strictly Jewish city.

It was with such reflections as these that we rode over the vast ruins and desolate plains, where no hut or human being is to be seen. The great port and channel of communication is now obliterated. No vessel rides in the distant bay, and nothing is heard but the sound of the rolling waves sending up a mournful dirge over all this desolation. It would almost break the heart of an enthusiastic artist to see the broken limbs of statues, and pieces of exquisitely-carved Corinthian capitals, trampled under his horse's feet, or lying embedded in sand and weeds. I was favoured with a sight of Mr.

Wood's sketches and diagrams, and was guided by him to some of his late discoveries. I shall not make reference to these just now, as I believe that he is preparing his works for early publication, when the public will be made acquainted with these important explorations. Returning to the station we visited the old Byzantine castle, the "great mosque," or St. John's Church, as it is called, and there can be no doubt, from the form and architecture, that it was an early Christian church. The railway passes under the old Roman aqueduct, of which a great many of the lofty arches are still standing. We got the return train at 4 P.M., and were back in Smyrna at 7 P.M., thence—"*partant pour la Syrie !*"

CHAPTER IV.

THREE steamers touch each week at Smyrna, all bound for the coast of Syria—the Austrian, French, and Russian boats. The charge for first-class passage is 260 francs to Jaffa (Joppa). After some consideration I selected the Russian boat, as I was told it would get into Jaffa two days before the others. I regretted that I did not take the Austrian boat, as we had upwards of 200 Russian-Greek pilgrims, and the like number of sheep on deck.

We sailed on the 7th November. There were only two other first-class passengers on board, a Russian nobleman and his lady, and but for their presence, I confess, I should have had my misgivings. Many of these Russian pilgrims had been three months on their journey, and during that time had never washed or changed their clothes. They had the most forbidding looks I ever saw— the women amusing themselves all day hunting in each other's hair, and the men relieving their smoke occasionally with the same occupation. They turned out, however, a very quiet and inoffensive people, entirely under subjection, and they often excited our pity and compassion.

These Russian boats are commanded by officers of the navy, and our captain was a good type of the educated Russian, speaking English and French fluently, a very gentlemanly man, and evidently a cool and excellent sailor. The weather for five days was very fine. Our first stoppage was at Chio, or Scio, where we remained three hours, but did not land, and the next day we anchored off Rhodes. We did not land here, but had an excellent view of this old stronghold of the Knights of St. John. A considerable portion of the walls and fortifications are still standing, but no one could point out the site of the "great Colossus." From the deck of the boat the view of the town is fine and picturesque, with the pretty white villas behind, stretching up along the face of the hill. We sailed at 5 P.M., and next day passed the island of Cyprus on our right, and at midnight reached Marsina, where a considerable trade in cotton has lately sprung up. We left in the morning, and on the next evening anchored off Alexandretta, the port of Aleppo, and near to the pass which divides Asia Minor from Syria, through which Alexander led his army when he fought the

famous battle of Issus. We left the same evening,
and on the morning of the 12th November anchored
off Ladikiyah. This, we are told, was an important
town in the time of the Phœnicians, but is now a
poor miserable place, and only kept alive by its small
trade in tobacco, and a little silk and cotton. We
did not land, but were informed that the 4,000 inhabitants are in a poverty-stricken state, and that the
fine and fertile country around lies in comparative
neglect. We left at noon, and towards evening had
a heavy storm of wind and rain—the first of the
Syrian winter storms—a sad night for the women
and children on deck, wet, sick, and sorrowful. I
could scarcely turn into my cabin, so sad was the
scene; and yet it was but little to what we had yet
to see of their sufferings. We arrived at Tripoli at
5 P.M., took in a little cargo, and sailed again at
10 P.M. This "triple city" has lost all its Phœnician and Roman importance, but has lately begun
to revive, and a considerable trade has sprung up
in cotton, silk, and tobacco. The town is finely
situated, and the gardens and buildings look well
from the harbour. Next day we got the first sight
of the snow-capped range of the Lebanon, and
should have enjoyed the scenery very much, but
that the rain and storm still continued, and the

sufferings of the pilgrims and other deck passengers drew upon our sympathies.

I was thankful when, on the morning of the 13th November, we got into Beyrout. I landed immediately, as we were to remain here twenty-four hours, and went to the Oriental Hotel. I was recommended to Mr. Bassone, the proprietor, a Maronite, and an excellent type of these active, industrious people, kind, courteous, and obliging. I called at the British consul's, was well received by Mr. Aldridge, and got a file of late English papers—the first I had seen for a month. I delivered my introductions to Dr. Bliss, and to Dr. Thomson, author of the "Land and the Book," and spent the day in going over the schools and college. But as I shall be here again for three days on my way back, I shall reserve my remarks till I am better acquainted with the place.

The vessel was to sail at 7.30 A.M. next morning, and when I got up at 6 A.M. to go on board, a fearful storm of wind and rain was raging, and I was doubtful if I could reach the ship. I found two or three passengers waiting to embark, and after a little squabble with the boatmen, and a promise of extra backsheesh, we got off, and safely on board, with only a slight ducking, just a few minutes before the vessel sailed. This day was the worst we had experienced. The wind had increased to a gale, the lightning flashed, and the rain fell in torrents. Women and children, rugs and mattresses, rolled from side to side. The children were past crying, but it was heartrending to see their sufferings. We had passengers and cargo for Acre; but when we came off that stormy point, the S.W. wind was blowing the white foam over the battlements. Two vessels had dragged their anchors, and were wrecked on the sands of the bay. The captain, I think very wisely, gave this dangerous point a wide berth, and ran across the bay under the shelter of Mount Carmel, and anchored off Haiffa about 4 P.M. Here the Acre, or Akka, passengers were landed. The storm still raging outside, the captain came into the cabin, looking, I thought, pale and careworn, and remarked to me, with a forced smile, "I expect we are going to have a row. If this weather continues, it is impossible we can lie off Jaffa, and I cannot take these deck passengers on to Alexandria, and must land them here, and I think it will be your better plan to land here also. You will find comfortable accommodation at the Convent, and can there make arrangements for your journey to Jerusalem." I was not in any way prepared for a land journey of five or six days, and decided at once that I would go on to Alexandria, in the event of not being able to land at Jaffa. After a time he decided that he would remain till next day, to see if any change took place in the weather; and, fortunately for us all, about noon next day the barometer began to rise and the storm to abate, and by 4 P.M. we were able to run across the bay to Acre, to land and take in some cargo, and get under way again at 9 P.M. The captain determined to lie off Jaffa, if possible, and get rid of his live cargo.

At daylight on the 16th we approached Jaffa, and found that the Austrian boat had gone on without being able to land her mails and passengers. The wind was still high, with heavy sea. Our captain, however, seemed determined to get rid of his passengers at any risk, and came to anchor about one and a half miles off the town, and here we had an example of what these hardy Arab boatmen are capable of doing. There is no harbour, but an open coast exposed to the S. and S.W. winds. The gale was still blowing hard, and the sea rolling over the broken beach. The Arab boatmen came off as soon as we anchored; and I shall never forget the scene of landing those sick, weary, and worn pilgrims. All was now chaos and confusion. A com-

panion-ladder was quite out of the question. Four
boats lay off both sides of the vessel, at the main
and fore chains. The vessel was rolling, gunwales
under. These powerfully muscular Arabs found
their way up the sides of the vessel like cats, threw
the luggage into the boats, and getting hold of the
women by the neck and legs, watched the roll of the
vessel, and, without any ceremony, literally pitched
them over the side into the boats, their own bundles
and mattresses breaking their fall, while others of
the crew stood on the gunwale of the boats to keep
them from dashing against the sides of the vessel.
For nearly an hour I stood witnessing this distressing scene. I remained on board till the decks were
cleared, and landed with the other cabin passengers,
without inconvenience beyond a slight ducking.

I remained at Jaffa only a few hours, visited the
only school I found here, conducted by Miss Arnott,
an earnest, zealous woman, who only complained that
she had not the means to do the work she saw before
her. I found that the British consul, who is also the
banker here, had gone to look after a vessel wrecked
off Gaza. I went round by "the house of Simon
the tanner, by the seaside," the lower part of which
is now a mosque; like all show places in Syria, it
is very apocryphal. It is sufficient for us to know

that St. Peter visited this town, and taught here that invaluable lesson to Jew and Gentile of universal Christian brotherhood. The town of Jaffa is finely situated, and has a pretty and pleasant appearance . from the sea, as it rises in terraces along the face of a conical-shaped hill; but this favourable impression is dispelled as soon as we land on the shore, where we find the true type of the foul and neglected Turco-Arab city. It was a great disappointment to find all our early associations and ideas connected with this ancient city pass away "like the baseless fabric of a vision"—to find no harbour and no trade, where "Hiram, king of Tyre, sent by sea the wood from Lebanon on floats to Joppa, from whence it was carried to Jerusalem." There was no encouragement for us to tarry here. The rain had washed all dirt and offal into the narrow, unpaved streets, and it was with difficulty that we could pick out steps without sinking ankle deep in filth. Two of my fellow-passengers, a Russian-Greek and his wife, on a pilgrimage to Jerusalem, were anxious to proceed on their journey; and as I was equally desirous to get forward, we arranged to proceed at once. The lady could not ride, or "had no side saddle": we therefore sent for the American, who has a small covered van that he runs between Jaffa and Jerusalem. We engaged it at once for ourselves at twenty francs each, and at 2 P.M. started for Ramleh, where we proposed stopping the night.

I may mention here that horses may be hired from Jaffa to Jerusalem at the same money, twenty francs each ; and as the distance is about thirty-two miles, a good rider in fair weather may do the journey easily in seven to eight hours. I was very glad, however, that we took the conveyance, as we were able to read and talk quietly of the scenes around us. Our coachman was the proprietor of the conveyance, and one of the " American colony " that *settled* near Jaffa some years ago. These men were of a pious turn of mind, and were led to the belief that the return of the Jews to Palestine, under the government of their Messiah, was at hand, and with that " calculation " and devotion which characterises the New England men, they took the opportunity of being the first on the field, that they might come in for a fair share of the temporal and spiritual advantages that would follow this advent. These deluded men invested their all in this speculation, and were pillaged, both by their own countrymen and the Arabs. There was another cause, more potent, to account for the collapse of this enterprise, viz., the absence of a healthy government, and the presence of

corruption and injustice, of which the following is
an example. One of these settlers had bought a
fine young Arab horse, for which he paid some sixty
dollars. The animal was stolen from his premises
at night, and after a strict search throughout the
country was discovered in the possession of a native
who was offering it for sale. An application was
made to the sheik, or judge, of the district; the
evidence was clearly in favour of the American; but
the Arab swore that the horse was his, and being a
man of some influence he got the ear of the judge,
who decided the case in his favour. An appeal was
made to the American consul at Jerusalem, and the
horse was impounded and kept at the expense of the
prosecutor. Some months had elapsed when we
met the American on his way to Jerusalem to make
a further appeal to his own or the British consul for
the restoration of his property. While he was re-
lating his troubles to us, and I expressing some
indignation, this good man never allowed an angry
or vindictive word to escape his lips. Our conductor
was a man of the same quiet and cool temperament,
kind and considerate, and did everything he could
for our comfort. On leaving the filthy streets of the
city, the change was something enchanting, and we
walked for some time among the orange gardens

before we got into our conveyance. Nothing can
look more rich and beautiful than this outskirt of the
plains of Sharon. These gardens supply Jerusalem
and many other places in the interior, also passing
vessels, with oranges, lemons, apricots, bananas, and
other fruits, as well as an abundant supply of vegetables of all kinds. After passing this beautiful and
fertile land we came on a comparatively uncultivated sandy plain, until we reached Ramleh, at 5 P.M.
Our guide and driver was well known to and respected by the monks, and we were at once admitted,
and shown to clean and comfortable bedrooms, while
they were preparing our dinner, which was served
up by one of these quiet and courteous brothers.

This was my first night in one of these so-called
religious establishments. I have my own opinion
about the folly of men shutting themselves out from
the world and dreaming out their existence. But
if I speak of these monks as kindly hosts and pur-
veyors I have nothing but good to say, and pleasant
recollections of their hospitality.

The following morning, as soon as it was daylight, I made my way through the olive-groves,
to the fine Saracenic tower, and from its balcony
had a splendid view of the country round, from
Lydda, where St. Peter "came down to the saints,"

and over the mountains of Judæa, and along the plains of Sharon, down to the Mediterranean, and looking down on the village of Ramleh in its thicket of olive, carob; and palm trees, and hedges of cacti. The morning was bright and balmy, and after a light breakfast we gave the attendant brother what he was pleased to call a "too handsome gratuity," and left with light and buoyant hearts. Towards noon we entered the pass or gorge of Babel Wady, and at a little Arab *café* by the roadside rested and had our lunch under the shadow of a tree. And now commenced the rugged ascent towards Jerusalem. This was once one of the worst roads in Palestine. They are now constructing a new road, and in a short time we may hear of coaches running daily between Jaffa and Jerusalem.

The rise from the plain to Jerusalem is 2,600 feet, and the ascent being sometimes very abrupt, we were glad to get out to lighten the burden of the horses. As we gain the heights of these "mountains of Judæa," the scenery is wild, barren, and desolate. Some Arab villages are seen perched on the face of the hills, like deserted birds' nests. No vestige of vegetation, and scarcely a human being to be seen; and we naturally ask ourselves, Can this be the "promised land?—a land flowing with milk

and honey "—a land so rich that the description, by
Josephus, of its vast revenue and resources seems
almost fabulous.   But this apparent mystery is
partly explained by what we have said in reference
to the extraordinary fertility of the "plains of
Sharon," and to other great plains to which we shall
have occasion to refer in future chapters.

Before making the last ascent we rested at a
fine spring of water, near the Vale of the Kedron,
where tradition says David slew the lion. On a
lofty peak to the left is a mosque over the reputed
tomb of Samuel. We were now looking out
anxiously for the first sight of the Holy City, but
this has been almost eclipsed by the hospice, church,
and hospital of the Russian convent, covering some
acres of ground, or rather rock, and forming one of
the most prominent objects round Jerusalem.   It
was only when we were within ten minutes of the
city that we saw the old Jaffa Gate and the citadel
and tower of David. My companions were bathed
in tears. No word was spoken : there are moments
when the heart is too full for words. If the field
of Marathon inspires one with patriotism, and the
ruins of Iona with devotion, the reader may judge
what must be the feelings of the Christian when he
has his first sight of Jerusalem.

I would have wished to enter the Holy City with my mind undisturbed; but when our luggage was laid out before the custom-house officers, the lady objected to have her boxes opened, which a little backsheesh might have kept shut, and consequently there was a great deal of abuse on the part of the lady and her husband, till I begged them to let the waiter of the hotel, who had come out to meet us, settle the matter with the official in the usual way. This was easily effected by opening only one or two cases and slipping a few piasters into his hand. If it be necessary to soothe one's conscience for "an act of bribery and corruption," it is easily done, as I believe this is the only form in which these servants of this corrupt government are re-munerated. We parted with our worthy New England friend with a grateful sense of his kind-ness and attention on the journey. We entered the city by the Jaffa Gate, winding our way over rough and slippery boulders, through dirty narrow streets, and under long dark arches, by the "Via Dolorosa" to the Mediterranean Hotel, near the Damascus Gate, where we were very comfortably lodged.

My first impression of Jerusalem was a kind of disappointment which I cannot well describe. It was not the "City of David" and home of our faith that I had long been picturing to myself, and so ardently longed that I might live to see. And I could not in any way identify it with our common Christianity. I read portions of the Old and New Testament that bore upon its history, but could not account for my frame of mind, till the light broke in upon me, that the time had come " that we shall neither in this mountain nor yet at Jerusalem worship the Father. God is a Spirit, and they that worship him must worship in spirit and in truth," whether on the bleak mountain sides of the north, or on the sunny slopes of the Himalaya ;

" Or haply in some cottage far apart,
    Our God may hear well pleased the language of the soul,
    And in his book of life the inmates poor enrol."

" Wherever two or three are gathered together in His name, there will He be in the midst of them." I am now more than ever convinced of the violence that men do to the pure and simple worship of the Father, in attempting to give that worship a favoured home, whether at Rome or at Jerusalem.

A gentleman of great intelligence and observation, who had resided for a length of time in Jerusalem and travelled through most of Palestine, said to me, " You must employ your first week in seeing and believing everything in and about this city, for every day you remain after will throw more and more doubt on your mind, till nothing will seem real but the blue sky above and the eternal hills around." It took me less than a week to go through the process of disillusion. Yet the fictions and follies of superstition concerning particular places do not affect the feeling that we are upon—

> "Those holy fields,
> Over whose acres walked those blessed feet
> Which, eighteen hundred years ago, were nailed,
> For our advantage, on the bitter cross."

CHAPTER V.

BEFORE I proceed to describe what I saw in Jerusalem, the reader will be pleased to accompany me to Hebron, and also to the Jordan and Dead Sea.

For the first journey three of us made arrangements with a dragoman, a very active, good-tempered, and intelligent young man. Abraham was a Jew proselyte, educated at the school of Bishop Gobat, to all appearance a good and sincere Protestant. He spoke good English, also professing French, German, and Italian, besides his native Arabic. All arrangements were left to him to furnish every necessary at 35s. each, that is £5 5s. in all, for two days. There was no further guide necessary, except a man to look after the horses, who was mounted on a donkey, and carried some of our provisions. The four horses on which we and the dragoman were mounted turned out safe and excellent animals, and we had a very pleasant journey.

The distance from Jerusalem to Hebron is about

twenty miles, and was accomplished, including stoppages, in seven hours. We left Bethlehem on our left till our return next day, and proceeded through a wild mountainous country, sometimes climbing up the mountain side between great boulders, or along slippery limestone declivities, where no animal but a goat could have kept a footing, or the sure-footed half-Arab horses we rode, finding it best to leave the reins slack on their necks, and let them take their own way.

As we approached the Valley of Hebron, or Eshcol, the vegetation increased, and the slopes of the mountains were terraced with vineyards, fig-trees, and olives. The season was now past, but in spring and during the vintage the scene must be rich and beautiful. Before entering the town we made a short detour to see the so-called Oak of Abraham, under the shadow of which the patriarch is said to have sat when visited by the angels. It may be a lineal descendant of the patriarchal oak, and is now sole representative of its family. It may be any age from two to three hundred years; a venerable tree of more than 20 feet circumference. It has a smaller leaf than our English oak, and is, I believe, known to botanists as the terebinth oak.

We reached Hebron at 4 P.M., and put up at

the house of a Jew, a very wretched and uncomfortable place. There were no windows in the house, but wooden boards for shutters; the bare little room into which we were shown overlooked a stagnant pool, with the Mohammedan buryingground beyond. Having still two hours of daylight, we started at once to see the great mosque over the Cave of Machpelah. We were not allowed to approach within forty paces of the main entrance. One of our party, attempting to advance up the passage leading to the Haram, was rudely insulted and called back, and our dragoman requested us not to advance any farther, as he could not guarantee our safety, for the Moslems of Hebron are the most fanatical in Palestine. We were guided round to some high ground to the north, where we were able to look down on the building, and to gather a fair idea of its construction. It forms a quadrangle of about 200 feet long by 120 feet wide. With the help of our glasses we were able to see those great cyclopean stones in the lower part of the wall which mark so distinctly the early Jewish portion of the building; the remainder of the building is clearly a mixture of Christian and Saracenic architecture.*

* The reader who may be desirous to pursue this inquiry further will find full details of the interior in the able work of Mr.

·I may here deviate from my first resolution, to confine myself only to what came under my own observation, and devote a few lines to the remarks of Dean Stanley, when he accompanied the Prince of Wales through the building. After great difficulty and tedious negotiation, the Prince and suite were permitted to examine the interior under an escort of soldiers. After describing the general character of the building, the original Jewish walls, and mediæval Christian and Mohammedan additions, the Dean states that they were shown over the so-called shrines of the Patriarchs. In the first chapels, or recesses, outside the mosque, were pointed out the tombs of Abraham and Sarah. "There was a groan from the guardians as they entered the shrine, and the chief turned to our party and remarked that the prince of any other nation should have passed over his dead body sooner than enter; but to the son of the Queen of England they were willing to accord even this privilege;" and, he might have

Fergusson, on the "Architecture of Palestine," and in the learned researches of Dean Stanley, who accompanied the Prince of Wales to this place. As far as I am aware, the only persons from this country that have been admitted into the building have been the Prince and his suite, Mr. Fergusson, and that eccentric young nobleman, the Marquis of Bute, and from them we gather very little information of the real tombs of the Patriarchs.

added, for the English blood spilt in their defence in the Crimea. They found these tombs merely ceno-taphs, which might have been called by any other name; and were still left in ignorance of the real burying-places of the patriarchs. In another part of the mosque were pointed out the tombs of Isaac and Rebekah, to which they were refused admission. In other recesses were the shrines of Jacob and Leah, and in a detached chamber they were shown the tomb of Joseph. This latter required some explanation, as both Jew and Moslem point out the tomb of Joseph in the vale of Shechem, but the tradition at Hebron is that the body was afterwards removed here, that it might lie with the other patriarchs. These cenotaphs rest on mere Moslem tradition; and if the caves containing the bodies of the patriarchs were under this edifice, they have long since disappeared, otherwise we should have had some record of them during the many years the building was in the hands of the early Christians, and subsequently in possession of the Crusaders. The royal visitors saw nothing of the "Caves of Machpelah;" and beyond examining the architecture, and comparing the different styles and probable dates of its construction, they made no discoveries, nor had any great advantage beyond ourselves. Notwithstanding, I must confess my chagrin at being thus rudely repulsed from the building.

I have lived long enough amongst Hindoos and Mohammedans to make every allowance for their prejudices and fanaticism, and would neither ask nor expect them to make any great sacrifice of these to gratify mere curiosity; but these sheiks and mollahs know as well as we do that the tombs of the patriarchs, and all that appertain to the Old Testament history, are as sacred to the Jew and Christian as they can possibly be to the Mohammedans, and when intelligent men seek to gratify a religious desire or archæological curiosity, it is simply a gratuitous insult to deny them this privilege. It cannot be a matter of religious scruples, as the Mosque of Omar at Jerusalem, and that of Damascus, and other equally "holy places," have been thrown open to all who can afford to pay a fee of ten francs.

There is no city in Palestine, with the exception of Jerusalem, so often referred to in sacred history as Hebron, and indeed it was a city of importance long before Jerusalem was known to fame; and notwithstanding our disappointments, our visit was a very gratifying one. After visiting the two ancient pools, which still form reservoirs for the

supply of water, over one of which David hanged
the murderers of Ishbosheth, we returned to our
quarters and had a very uncomfortable night.
One of our party, a restless dyspeptic individual,
would not lie down on the suspicious rugs that were
laid round the raised divan, but went round the
walls with his slipper, and every now and then,
just as we were getting into a little doze, we were
startled by a slap with this slipper against the wall,
and an exclamation, "I've killed another dozen!"
till at last, in self-defence, I was forced to get up and
light a cigar, and wait patiently for daylight. When
our dragoman came in we asked for some water to
refresh ourselves, but these miserable people, who
had driven a hard bargain with him, and had got
fifteen francs for the use of the bare walls of a room,
refused to give us even an earthen vessel to wash
our face in, "as it would be defiled." They are still
the same obstinate and "stiff-necked people." No
amount of suffering seems to subdue them; and
though they walk about here in dirt and rags, half
bent before the insolent Moslems, I am persuaded
that, if they had the power, they would be far more
fanatical and intolerant than the Mohammedans.
The Jews here, as in all parts of Palestine, are distinguished by their dress—a gabardine, or long

coarse coat, a felt hat, and long greasy ringlets,
hanging down their careworn checks.

We started soon after daylight, as we had a long
day's work before us. We went over the same
ground that we did the day before till we came to
the three great pools of Solomon, about half-way on
the journey to Jerusalem, where we rested and had
some refreshment. We again mounted, and riding a
little distance to the north, we saw the fountain
which supplies these great reservoirs. The largest of
these pools is about 380 feet long by 230 feet broad.
The lower two diminish in size. They are partly
excavated, and partly built; they are evidently of
Jewish construction, and probably as old as the
time of David or Solomon. There are still some
remains of the aqueducts and stone pipes that conveyed these waters to Jerusalem. We rode down to
the rich and now beautifully cultivated valley watered
from these pools, and laid out in gardens, which
belong to private persons—one of them, we were
told, to our Royal Prince Arthur.

Instead of retracing our steps, our dragoman took
us up by a valley to Bethlehem, where we arrived
soon after mid-day. The first and greatest object of
interest here is " the Church of the Nativity." One
has no great difficulty in believing this to be on or

near the spot where our Saviour was born; the
locality agrees with the sacred narrative. The
church, with its three convents, forms a prominent
object on the eastern ridge of the terraced hill on
which the town is situated. For the style of building I must refer the reader to "Fergusson's Architecture." As regards the ancient church, with its
long aisle and double rows of marble columns, and
decayed mosaics, its materials and style, much is
borrowed from the Romans, and no doubt dates
from the time of the Empress Helena. The building is portioned out to the three rival churches,
Greek, Latin, and Armenian, who seem to have lost
sight of the great essentials of Christianity, love and
charity towards our neighbours. Not long ago, our
guide informed us, a very serious quarrel arose
between two of the rival sects. One had intruded
the end of his carpet on the sacred precincts of the
other, and was ordered to remove it; angry words
ensued, and each being backed up by his own devout
and orthodox companions, a disgraceful row took
place, which ended in bloodshed. From one of the
chapels we were led down a flight of dark steps, and
by a long, dimly-lighted passage entered the "Chapel
of the Nativity," partly hewn out of the rock and
lighted with numerous lamps. At one end is the

BETHLEHEM

small *sanctum*, with a marble slab under an altar, and on it a silver star encircled by a Latin inscription, the English of which is, "Here Jesus Christ was born of the Virgin Mary." Near to this is the "Chapel of the Manger," which is represented by a marble trough! It would be tedious to detail the various chapels and their traditions with which the mind is mystified; we shall therefore retrace our steps through these dark passages, amid glimmering lamps, where the most sacred events of Christianity are caricatured in gilt, tinsel, and coloured daubs of saints, till one feels inclined to shut their eyes to the tawdry display, and think only of those "good tidings of great joy which shall be to all people." The most authentic and unquestioned objects in these vaults are the tomb of St. Jerome, and his study. The inspection of all these objects occupied us about an hour, when we ascended to the convent, and had some refreshment, and satisfied the good monk who attended us.

We mounted our horses and started for the "Cave of Adullam," a distance of three miles, a very tiresome and fatiguing journey, over rocks and precipices, just such a place as David and his "distressed and discontented" companions would fly to for refuge. The approach to it is something fearful,

F

and had it not been for the Arab guides we took
with us, we should never have found it out. We
were obliged to dismount and leave our horses behind, and to scramble up the face of the glen, often
on our hands and feet, and creeping under projecting
rocks, till we gained the mouth of the principal
cave. We had taken candles with us, which we
lighted when we got within. There are a succession
of caves, the one leading into the other, reminding
me of those limestone caves which I visited a quarter
of a century ago, on the southern coast of the Island
of Java, in which are found the edible birds'-nests,
except that the former had not those long stalactites
hanging down like great chandeliers from the roof,
and sparkling in the light of our torches. Here
everything was dark, dismal, and suffocating. We
passed from one dark chamber into another, till our
Arab guides lost, or pretended to have lost, their
way back to the main entrance. We were tired and
faint, and—like other Adullamites—I confess I felt
greatly relieved when we got out into the light and
open air.

Opposite to these caves, and beyond the valley,
rises the isolated and artificial-looking mountain
called the "Frank" or "Crusaders' Mountain."
Having still two hours of daylight, we mounted

our horses and rode across the wady, and up the
steep winding path that leads to the top of the
mountain. On gaining the summit, the view from
the flat plateau is among the widest and grandest
in Palestine. A portion of the Dead Sea and Valley
of the Jordan seems to lie at our feet, and the whole
range of the wilderness of Judea and the scenery
round Jerusalem are distinctly marked. From the
Roman ruins, and remains of old walls, it is clear
that this must have been an important Roman
station, and it is said to be the burying-place of
Herod the Great, whose body was brought here
from Jericho. We had a very rough ride back to
Bethlehem, and nearly lost our way. It was now
getting dusk, and it was still from seven to eight
miles to Jerusalem. Fortunately we had a bright
moonlight and fine evening, and at a hard canter
we got home before the Jaffa Gate was closed,
which is the only one kept open after sunset till
8 P.M.

The next day (Saturday) I made arrangements to
join another party on Monday, to proceed to the
Dead Sea and the Jordan. On Sunday we wor-
shipped for the first time, in Christ's Church, on
Mount Zion. The service was read by Bishop
Gobat, and the sermon preached by the Rev. Mr.

Bailey. We spent the afternoon on Mount Olivet, to which one returns again and again with renewed interest.

We had been so well pleased with our smart young dragoman, Abraham Samuel, that at my suggestion my new companions engaged him to accompany three of us to the Dead Sea and the Jordan. The arrangement was £3 each, for a journey of three days, including food, servants, Bedouin guard, and all necessary expenses. We started on Monday morning at 8 A.M., and rode out by Bethlehem. As my two companions had not seen the Church of the Nativity, we stopped here for an hour, going over the scenes which I have already described. We also made a short detour to the Tomb of Rachel. No doubt has ever been entertained that this is the place where "Rachel died, and was buried, on the way to Ephrath, which is Bethlehem." The pillar of which Moses spoke has long been swept away, and now the spot is covered by a small dome and Mohammedan mosque, alike reverenced by Christian, Jew, and Moslem. We were now joined by our Bedouin escort, a chivalrous-looking young sheik, one of the sons of a well-known old chief, who has his residence between Jerusalem and the Jordan, and possesses great influence among the tribes inhabiting this district. Our equipage consisted of six horses, three mules, and a donkey, with tents, beds, cooking utensils, and all that was necessary for camp life.

Our journey to Mar Saba lay through the wilderness of Judea, a scene of desolation that no pen or pencil can depict : the white limestone crags and bleached hills of sand, and the few burnt-up roots of thistles, looked as if the blast of a furnace had passed over them. There was no road, and the common track led up and along the face of such slippery limestone slopes and rugged precipices that only a goat and wandering Bedouin could climb. There is nothing to relieve the wild and weary monotony till we reach the convent of Mar Saba. Our guide had brought the necessary pass from Jerusalem, and after a short parley from a little recess above the gate, we were admitted and conducted to a very comfortable chamber, with a raised divan round the walls, on which we spread our beds and quilts. While Abraham was preparing our dinner, one of the monks conducted us through the building to the tomb of its founder, St. Sabas,—the church, in which the brethren were engaged in devotion, and a chapel and charnel-house in which are shown the skulls of "10,000 martyrs," massacred by the Arabs. We expressed a wish to cross the valley to the opposite heights. A small door was opened overlooking an abrupt precipice, and a ladder passed out by which we descended till we got our footing below. We crossed the dry brook of the Kedron and ascended the face of the opposite hill. It was no easy task to get round and over the sharp points of rock, over which we assisted each other. But what a sight rewarded our labours! To the right and left was the deep gorge of the Kedron, and facing us the convent and detached cells of the monks, stuck like swallows' nests in the face of the glen, with stairs and passages cut out of the rock. There are about fifty of these monks, and they undergo a severe discipline, and are allowed no animal food, and look pale and careworn. It seem s a sad negation of life, and at variance with all the active principles of Christianity, a sort of asylum for the helpless and imbecile. We had a fine clear moonlight night, and before turning in we lighted our cigars and had a long stroll on the top of our dormitory. The deep shadows of the glen seemed deeper still. The scattered buildings around us, and rising over our heads with all their outlines distinctly marked by the bright moonlight, formed a scene of sublime grandeur rarely to be seen and never to be forgotten.

On the following morning, soon after daylight, we left the convent, with an acknowledgment for the kindness and attention of the brethren, and with some sorrow and sympathy for these poor dreaming isolated men. The scenes through which we passed were wild and desolate, no human habitation being within sight. We saw occasionally a flock of goats clinging to the mountain sides, and cropping the dry weeds that find shelter in the crevices of the rock, tended by a ragged savage-looking Bedouin, with his long-barreled gun slung over his shoulder. Skirting the deep gorge of the Kedron, and along the rugged sides of the mountain, we came in sight of the Dead Sea after a ride of two hours, and in one and a half hours more we reached its shores, lying nearly 1,400 feet below the level of the sea, so that we had descended from Jerusalem 5,000 feet. The thermometer stood at 85°, and the atmosphere was somewhat oppressive. The calm sea lay like a sheet of silver amidst these barren hills. We stripped, and entered its water, so transparent that one could see to any depth. Before we got in to our armpits we were carried off our feet, and obliged to strike out. One of our party made for a small island a

little way from the shore, but was clamorously called
upon to return, as there was a great depth of water,
and if any mishap had occurred, no power could
have saved him. We dismiss at once the fables
about "no living thing surviving on its surface," as
we saw both birds and vegetation around it. The
density of the water is about three times that of the
ocean, which will account for its buoyant power.
In paddling about I got a few drops in my eyes,
and for a few seconds I felt as if they were cut
out of my head. On coming out we felt a little
irritation on the skin, and as soon as we could dress
we mounted and hurried on to the Jordan to get a
fresh-water bath.

The ford at which the pilgrims bathe, and perhaps
the very place at which our Saviour was baptized, is
about an hour's ride from the Dead Sea, and no
doubt near to where the children of Israel crossed
"over against Jericho" (Joshua iii. 16). The
Jordan is not an attractive river. It winds through
high muddy banks, and has a brown, dirty appearance. The current at this point was very strong,
and we did not attempt to swim, and only walked in
as far as we considered safe, enjoying the cool,
refreshing bath. My companions filled their tin
cans with the water. I had too much work before

FORDS OF THE JORDAN

me thus to encumber myself. We now rode across
the dry, barren plain, a distance of five miles, to
Old Jericho, and found our tents pitched by the
fountain of Elisha, or, as it is now called, " Ain-es-
Sultan," from which flows a full clear stream,
watering a perfect forest of trees and shrubs, of
which no advantage is taken. The palmy days of
Jericho are long past, and not one tree is now to be
seen near the "City of Palms." We found this
spot in the hands of a few wandering Bedouins, who
only seek a little pasture for their flocks. The
second Jericho of Herod, referred to in the New
Testament, is about one and a half miles farther
down the valley. The site of both cities is very
doubtful. In the neighbourhood of our camp there
were four or five mounds, which are supposed to
'indicate the site of ancient Jericho. We went over
these, and found that Lieutenant Warren, R.E., had
sunk several shafts, but without any satisfactory
results. These mounds are evidently accumulations
of *débris,* but nothing was found but loose stones and
broken pottery.

Our intelligent dragoman had sent everything on
before us, and on our return we found our beds
arranged round the side of the tent, with a table in
the centre, and an excellent dinner of four or five

courses provided, commencing with well-seasoned
sago soup, and ending with bread-pudding and fruit
dessert. We were cautioned to keep our traps well
together, in case of the prowling Bedouins finding
something that struck their fancy, but I believe we
were perfectly safe in the hands of our young sheik.
In the morning, while they were striking the tents
and getting ready for departure, we rode south to
the small village and ruins of the Jericho of Herod,
but saw nothing of interest to indicate the presence
of any former city—nothing but the sad spectacle of
the total neglect of all the most precious gifts, for
nature has abundantly supplied every means to
make this valley one of the most fertile spots on
earth. The River Jordan has a fall of 600 feet
from the sea of Galilee to the Dead Sea, and in its
fall brings down as rich an alluvium as that of the
Nile, which, by the simplest process of irrigation,
might be carried over the whole plain between the
two seas, yielding crops of cotton, sugar-cane, and
grain of all kinds, sufficient for half a million of
inhabitants, where now there is nothing but a forest
of weeds, and a few wandering Bedouins. While in
this locality one's attention is naturally called to
the supposed sites of the "Cities of the Plain." I,
in common with many others who had their im-

pressions from early writers, supposed that these cities were to the south of the Dead Sea, and were doubtless engulfed in its waters. From late reading and observation, I have now formed a different opinion, and am inclined to think that the cities spoken of were in the fertile valley of the Jordan, to the north of the Dead Sea. If the reader will refer to the thirteenth chapter of Genesis, he will notice that "Lot lifted up his eyes, and beheld all the plain of Jordan, that it was well watered everywhere, before the Lord destroyed Sodom and Gomorrah, like to the land of Egypt," etc. And while Abraham went westward to Mamre, the rich valley of Hebron, "Lot chose him all the plain of Jordan, and pitched his tent towards Sodom." This hypothesis is strengthened by the fact that Abraham, looking down from the heights near Hebron, could " see the smoke of the country rising like the smoke of a furnace." The total destruction and disappearance of these cities may easily be accounted for by the miraculous agency described in the nineteenth chapter of Genesis. Nor need we look for the ruins of these cities anywhere in the Dead Sea.

If time and circumstances had permitted, we should have remained here for two or three days, and explored the caves and early Christian relics

on and around the Quarantania Mountain, which,
according to tradition, is the place of our Saviour's
temptation.   But this we were obliged to forego.
On leaving the plains we began our ascent, over
rocky precipices, and through the "Wilderness of
Judea," over which our Saviour and his apostles
must often have· trodden on..their way from the
Jordan to Jerusalem.   About mid-day we came to
a fountain of delicious water, where we spread
our carpet and had lunch.   A number of shep-
herds had brought their flocks to this refreshing
oasis, and pilgrims from Jerusalem to the Jordan
were enjoying their frugal meal of brown bread and
salt curd.   An hour and a half's farther ride brought
us to the little Arab village of Bethany, a scene of
sad disappointment.   There is not a single relic to
remind one of its importance in gospel history.
Through a few scattered mud huts we were led to a
deep vault, with a broken stone stair leading down
to a dark chamber, which we were told was the
tomb of Lazarus.   There is nothing in this place
to realise or exalt our ideas of the Divine miracle.
Neither is there in a large ruin pointed out as the
house of Mary and Martha.   It is sufficient to know
that near to this spot lived that family "whom
Jesus loved."   Soon after leaving the village we

rounded the eastern spur of Mount Olivet, and all
at once the city of Jerusalem burst upon our sight.
Here we dismounted and sent our horses on, and
stood for some time contemplating the scene, from
perhaps the very spot where our Saviour stood and
"wept over the city." From this spot the city
must have appeared then in all its splendour. We
wound our way slowly down the eastern declivity,
over that path by which our Saviour made his trium-
phal entry, described in the twenty-first chapter of
St. Matthew, crossed the valley of Jehoshaphat, and
entered the city by St. Stephen's Gate.

This was one of the pleasantest journeys I had in
Palestine. We were importuned for backsheesh, as
usual, by our young sheik and attendants. A trifle
satisfied all claims, and we parted very good friends.

CHAPTER VI.

I now commenced my survey of the Holy City, where I remained twenty days. For the convenience of my readers, I propose to take the first six days, and give a short sketch of each day's experience in "sight-seeing."

First in traditional importance is the Church of the Holy Sepulchre. It is a sad and melancholy exhibition. I should be sorry to repeat the stories I heard of the artifices and contrivances of the staff of priests that live here on the ignorance and credulity of their victims. Those Greek, Roman, and Armenian orgies are not only a scandal to Christianity, but are a check to the progress of evangelism in the East. One can scarcely feel surprised at the Jew and Mohammedan turning with contempt from such a system of superstition and idolatry as they see in this perverted Christianity. Round the porch, or outside entrance to the church, is an open market for the sale of consecrated articles, such as rosaries, crosses, beads, pictures, and images of saints, and other objects of superstitious reverence, recalling to mind the words of the prophet Jeremiah (vii. 11), "Is this house, which you call by my name, become a den of robbers?" and one might ask, has not this house, called "His Holy Sepulchre," been turned into toy-shops and showmen's booths?

Whatever may be the opinion of intelligent Greek and Latin priests on these exhibitions, there seems no mistake about the sincerity and devotion of those poor, dirty, and ragged pilgrims, who have made their way, after months of toil and privation, from the most distant parts of Russia, to worship at the so-called tomb of our Saviour. These men, women, and children, in a sort of religious stupor, may be seen in tears kissing the sacred spots, with a stupid and forlorn look, which excites more of pity than contempt. But I am keeping the reader too long at the door of the Holy Sepulchre. We enter the building from the south, by a high Byzantine gate, and the first object that arrests our attention is a platform, or divan, with a guard of Turkish soldiers to keep peace among the professors of that gospel which breathes brotherly love and charity in every line. There are within the walls of this building, which may be about 250 feet square, no less than thirty-seven objects professedly identified with the

suffering and resurrection of our blessed Lord. I
will only make reference to a few of them, which
recall events that are familiar to us all. The first
object shown by our guide was the "Stone of
Unction," a marble slab, before which the devout
were kneeling and pressing their lips on the bare
stone. Turning to the left, we were shown a round
cage· called the "Station of the Virgin," where
Mary stood while they were anointing the body
of Jesus. Turning inward under the great dome,
we reach the Holy Sepulchre, an oblong building of marble about 26 feet by 18 feet, within
which we are shown the "actual sepulchre of our
Lord." The slab which covers it serves as an
altar, and over it are suspended a great number
of silver and gilt lamps, shedding a dim light,
and giving awe, if not solemnity, to the scene.
There are moments when one would wish to
banish all scepticism; and here in this dim recess, and afterwards standing before the altar of
the cross on Calvary, the great events in the
sufferings of our Saviour rush upon the mind and
fill the heart to overflowing. Outside the sepulchre
I met a Latin priest who had been my fellow-
passenger from Beyrout to Jaffa, and in conversation with him I made some allusion to the

round aperture in the wall of the Sepulchre, from
which the holy fire that descends from heaven and
miraculously lights up the lamps round the Holy
Sepulchre is handed out to the multitude of de-
votees by the officiating priest. "This," he replied,
"is another of those frauds that the Greek Church
practise on their ignorant and bigoted dupes. It is
an insult to religion to call these men priests, they
are ignorant, grasping, and deceitful;" and with
strong emphasis, he concluded in these words: "It
is not a religion, but a humbug, and an insult to
Christianity." I could scarcely look in his face and
keep my gravity, it was so like the "kettle and
the pot," especially as I knew that for many centuries the Latin Church held and practised a like
belief, and that it is not many years since—after
a quarrel with the Greek Church, when they were
deprived of the privilege of using the holy fire—
they discovered it to be "a wicked and impudent
imposture." I do not see that it is much worse
than their "Loretto house," or their "winking
and bleeding virgins," and other equally extravagant "impostures." The description given by
various writers of the scenes that sometimes take
place on Easter eve, when the Greek pilgrims
rush to light their tapers at the "holy fire," is

G

something appalling.   They are often attended with
serious loss of life.

Proceeding onward, in a line with the Sepulchre,
and under a second dome, is the Greek church, the
largest and richest within the building, and highly
decorated with gilt screens, elaborate carvings, and
massive chandeliers.   In the centre of the aisle is a
circular slab, with a radiating star called the " centre
of the world," with a legend attached to it.   A semicircular corridor runs round this church, in which
there are a number of chapels and altars, which I
need not enumerate.   Descending from this corridor
by a flight of twenty steps, we are shown the place
of the discovery of the true cross, and where the
Empress Helena sat when it was discovered.   Near
to this an altar is pointed out, which is called, curiously enough," The Chapel of the Invention of the
Cross," and in its neighbourhood, the "Pillar of
Flagellation " and the "Prison of Christ."   Ascending from this, we pass three or four other chapels,
and arrive at the stair leading up to Golgotha.   This
is supposed to be a rock elevated some twenty feet
above the general level of the building.   There are
several chapels on this platform, but I shall only
refer to the principal one, on the east side, called
" The Chapel of the Elevation of the Cross."   This

is supposed to be raised over the rock which was "rent" at the time of the crucifixion, and which is shown by the Greek priest in attendance. In front of the altar is a circular hole of five inches diameter, showing where the cross is said to have been fixed in the earth; and on each side, a little behind, are two holes for the crosses of the two thieves. I have said that there are moments when one would wish to banish all scepticism, and this is one of them, but the incidents passing around you soon dispel every feeling of solemnity.

It was now about 3 P.M., and we waited to see the afternoon procession of the three Churches round the building to the various so-called sacred spots. The Greeks take the lead; officiating priests, and pilgrim-followers, carrying lighted tapers, proceed from their own church, stopping at each altar to chant a prayer. They are followed at a short interval by representatives of the Latin Church, lay and clerical; and immediately after them come the Armenians. They sometimes get inconveniently close upon each other, and while the Armenians are chanting their service in the Chapel of Golgotha with all the power of their lungs, the Latins are equally vociferous round the "Table of Unction," immediately below them. The services mingle together in the wildest discord, turning the sacred drama into a badly-arranged comedy, and banishing all idea of solemnity. Among the other improbable and extravagant objects within the building are shown the tombs of Adam and Melchizedek. But I should only tire the reader by reference to all the puerile attempts to concentrate within this building objects which must have been spread over the whole of the ancient city and its neighbourhood. The whole is a mass of incongruity, producing nothing but sorrow and shame in the minds of simple Christians who witness such perversion of that pure and spiritual worship taught to the woman of Samaria by the Messiah, " God is a Spirit, and they that worship him must worship him in spirit and in truth " (John iv. 24). The building, from an artistic point of view, has no attractions: all is smoke, dirt, and dilapidation.

I visited this building again and again, and am still at a loss to describe its appearance. The best view of the exterior is from the open court on the south, by which we enter. There we recognise at once the Christian mediæval architecture: the pointed arch and sculptured portals, with the great tower—all the work of the Crusaders. This fine tower, which originally consisted of five or six stories, is now reduced to nearly half of its original height, and is in a neglected and ruinous state. Behind this rises the great dome, which covers the Holy Sepulchre, now in course of repair; Greek artists are employed in the interior, daubing it over with glaring colours and tinsel in the worst taste of modern Greek art, against which our contempt is aggravated by the knowledge that the privilege to execute these tawdry decorations led to that quarrel between France and Russia —the representatives of the two great religious factions—which formed an excuse for the sanguinary conflicts and calamitous events of the Crimean war.

Continuing the view eastward, we notice the lesser dome, which covers the Greek church; and passing on to the extreme east are the chapels on Calvary: the whole forming a patchwork of disjointed buildings consisting of convents, chapels, and galleries, without order, beauty, or design.

With regard to the authenticity of the site of the Tomb and Place of Crucifixion, there are conflicting opinions and speculations, to which I shall slightly refer when I come to speak of the topography of the ancient city and walls of Jerusalem, although it cannot be of the slightest interest from

a purely Christian point of view, as nothing can
be more evident than the marked neglect, or
obliteration and absence of all allusion to the so-
called holy places, by the apostles and their immediate followers, which seems so perfectly con-
sistent with our ideas of a universal Christian
faith, and that experience which we have of the
proneness of human nature to fall back into
material and idolatrous worship.

We returned to our hotel through the Via Dolorosa, another of those traditional places which came
into note many centuries after the events to which
they refer. Soon after leaving the Church of the
Sepulchre we enter a narrow, dirty, and ill-paved
street. This is the Via Dolorosa; and here may
be seen the Greek and Latin priests conducting
their votaries to the different "stations" to which
is attached some event connected with the crucifixion. Here the Saviour wiped his bleeding brow.
A stone in the wall of a house is worshipped as the
place where the Saviour, fainting under the weight
of the cross, leaned his shoulder. Winding our
way through this narrow street towards St. Stephen's Gate, we come to "the arch of the Ecce
Homo." This modern arch, which spans the
narrow street, is supposed to be near the house

of Pilate, and where he presented our Lord to the people, and said, "Behold the man!" These are all comparatively modern Arab buildings; the street could not have had an existence at the time of the events which it is thus sought to perpetuate. No miracle in the Eastern churches is greater than that of leading their votaries to the belief that these are the material objects, and this the way by which the Saviour was led to crucifixion.

The next day was set apart to visit the Mosque of Omar, and the other objects of interest, on what is called the Haram esh-Sherif, or noble sanctuary, a platform of 1,500 feet running north and south, overlooking the Valley of Jehoshaphat, and 900 feet from east to west. Our useful dragoman, Abraham, had procured us the necessary authority for admission here, as well as to the Citadel and Tower of David, at a charge of ten francs each person.

There is no doubt entertained that within the area of the Haram stood the ancient Temple of Jerusalem, but I shall not enter upon that subject till I have taken the reader over the objects that are now to be seen. I should mention that, until the Crimean war, this place was shut against all

but the "faithful," and for a Jew or Christian to
enter would be at the risk of his life. Even now
many of the good old conservative Moslems see in
the change "the narrow end of the wedge," and
look with jealousy on a privilege which in their
eyes amounts to sacrilege.

We entered by a gate at the north-west corner,
accompanied by an official with sword and semi-
military costume, and were led to the raised platform on which the Mosque stands, where we put
off our shoes, and were supplied with slippers, and
taken charge of by the old sheik who has the care
of the Mosque, a fine venerable-looking old man,
who, after shaking hands with us all round, asked
us for a snuff. My Highland countrymen would
have thought us a very unsocial lot not to have
a "sneishin' mull" among us, to cement our
friendship. Having seen that gem of Saracenic
architecture, the Taj Mahal at Agra, and other
monuments of the taste and wealth of the emperors
of India, I confess I was a little disappointed at
the first close inspection of this building. It
seemed, like everything else in the hands of the
Turks, dirty and neglected. The beautiful Damascus tiles and the arabesque colouring round
the frieze and outer wall were much broken and

dilapidated, and neither outside nor within did I see anything to be compared with even what remains of the beautiful Alhambra of Granada. It has been highly praised by all the most eminent architects who have seen it as "a thing of beauty;" and, viewed from every point around the city, the magnificent dome and imposing ·form and situation of the building cannot fail to strike every one who looks on it with admiration.

On entering the building, one is at a loss to recognise the style and period of the architecture. We see in the arches and columns a great deal that reminds us of the Mosque of St. Sophia at Constantinople, and other early Byzantine buildings, elaborated with later Saracenic or Arabesque colouring and ornament. The columns, like those of St. Sophia, are Græco-Roman, and are doubtless the remains of some earlier temple. From these indications, I am inclined to fall in with the views of Mr. Fergusson, in relation to the date and character of the so-called Mosque of Omar, viz., that it is an early Byzantine structure, and one of the four Christian edifices mentioned by several of the early Christian writers. These were "the Church of the Sepulchre," now the Mosque of Omar; the "Basilica of Constantine," the "Church

of Golgotha," and the "Church of St. Mary."
All these Mr. Fergusson places on the site of the
present platform, but outside the walls of the
Temple of Herod. And if the vaults lately discovered by Captain Warren, to the north-east of
the Mosque, could be fully examined, the fact
might be established that these are the remains of
the Basilica of Constantine, and thus afford a
perfect key to Mr. Fergusson's theory; but until
we have the means and full permission to excavate
in and around the Haram platform, these questions
cannot be settled. Those who are opposed to the
theory of Golgotha and the Sepulchre being to the
north-east of the Temple, and hold to the later
traditions of the present site, on Akra, say that
the Crusaders found it here, and having no doubt
of the authenticity of the place, built the present
Church of the Holy Sepulchre over the real tomb
of our Saviour. These arguments will have no
weight by the side of present investigations, as they
are more the result of sentiment than of impartial
knowledge. If we admit the place of crucifixion to
be north of the temple, we know what would follow.
The Mohammedans took possession of all places
held sacred by Jews and Christians, and appropriated most of them to the worship of their own

faith, forbidding both Jew and Christian to
approach these places. An ignorant and superstitious priesthood would naturally seek a Calvary
and Tomb of their own; and being permitted by
the Mohammedans to establish their ordinances
in the Christian quarters of the old city, would
draw the pilgrims round these so-called holy places.
So that what began in a well-intentioned "religious fraud," was received a few centuries later
as an established fact. As such, the Crusaders,
on entering Jerusalem, accepted the site unquestioned, and built the present "Church of the
Holy Sepulchre." I find it quite impossible to
reconcile this belief with all I have seen and
read of the subject, and feel convinced that this
so-called sepulchre stood in the midst of the old
city.

It may save the reader some trouble if I quote
a few lines from the fifth book and sixth chapter
of Josephus's "Wars of the Jews." He says: "The
city was built on two hills, which were divided by
a valley: the one was called the citadel of King
David, the other hill was called Akra, or stronghold, joining the lower city; and over against this
there was a third hill, parted by a valley: which
was afterwards filled up, and joined the city to the

Temple." The "two hills" were clearly what. are now called Mounts Zion and Akra, and the "third hill" was Mount Moriah, on which the Temple stood. If, therefore, the present Akra be that referred to by Josephus, which exactly answers the above description, the present "Church of the Sepulchre" stands in the centre of the ancient city, and cannot be either the Tomb or the Place of Crucifixion; but the "holy fraud" may be palliated, if not pardoned, in those whose credulity and devotion can admit the legend of the holy house of Mary being carried by angels from Nazareth to Loretto. I may mention one more circumstance which shakes our belief in the truth of these traditions. There is no cave under the slab and altar of the so-called sepulchre, and the place marked by the cross and the rent in the rock is at an elevation of twenty-five feet from the floor of the church; but there is nothing in the description given by the Evangelists to lead us to suppose that Golgotha was on an elevation: it was more likely to be where Mr. Fergusson has placed it, on the north-east slopes of Mount Moriah. The reader will, I trust, pardon this digression, on account of the great interest every Christian must feel on this subject, and return with me to the Mosque of Omar.

In the centre of the building, and immediately
under the beautiful dome, we are shown the
"Sacred Rock," which occupies a space fifty-five
feet in diameter, and stands about six feet above
the pavement of the mosque. We were led below,
by a flight of steps, to a vault under the rock, and
could see what appears to be the natural rock over
our heads. On stamping with the feet a hollow
sound is produced, and we are told the legend of
the rock being suspended in the air, and are shown
the footprints of Mohammed, where he last touched
the earth before his ascent to heaven, and the hand-
prints of the angel Gabriel, who held the rock down
as it was ascending with the prophet! There are
many other objects here equally marvellous, but,
after the "inventions" in the Church of the
Sepulchre, we must not say too much on the credulity of the followers of Mohammed.

Leaving the "Dome of the Rock," we were conducted along the Haram platform to the Mosque
of Aksa, on the south-west side of the platform.
Some writers of guide-books, and others, led away
by mediæval traditions, have assumed this to be
the "Church of the Virgin," referred to by early
Christian writers as having been built by Justinian.
There are strong evidences against this assump-

tion. First, in its architecture, which is evidently Mohammedan, raised on Jewish substructures; and secondly, if this is the site of the Temple, which it will not be difficult to prove, we know that the Temple was held accursed by the early Christians, who believed that the doom pronounced against it, that "not one stone of it should remain upon another," must be carried out.

We know scarcely anything of the site of the Temple, from the destruction of Jerusalem by Titus to the Mohammedan conquest, but then some light is indirectly thrown on the subject. The Moslems hold all places and objects connected with the Bible as sacred as do the Jews; and we may reasonably infer that their first inquiry, on entering Jerusalem, would be after the site and ruins of the Temple, on which they would most assuredly erect their first mosque. We must therefore abandon the idea that El Aksa was a Christian church before the Crusaders entered Jerusalem, when, guided by mistaken tradition, and totally ignorant of the early topography of the city, they claimed this mosque as the " Church of St. Mary," referred to by early Christian writers, and dedicated it to the Virgin, and placed it under the protection of the Knights Templars.

The building occupies a space of about 300 feet by 200 feet, on the south-west of the Haram platform. The whole substructure is of that massive style known as Phœnician or Jewish, and some of it may be as early as the time of Solomon. The superstructure, raised on these foundations, up to the dome, is such a mixture of Roman, Saracenic, and Christian architecture, that it is difficult to assign it to any date. I must confess to only a vague recollection of passing through vaults, between walls of massive bevelled stones, of columns and piers of cyclopean dimensions, a succession of aisles, surmounted by a Saracenic dome, ornamented with Arabesque. And although I have all this in my mind's eye, it is so undefined that I cannot convey to the reader any correct idea of this mass of mixed and incongruous architecture. It is not, however, its early and later history of a mosque, or its adaptation and occupation as a Christian church by the Crusaders, that gives this building such peculiar interest, but the all-absorbing question, Is this the site of the Temple of Solomon and Herod? And here I shall briefly refer to my own readings, and the opinion I have formed on the subject.

We will at once dismiss the assumption that the

Temple stood in the centre of the present platform,
and that the Moslem "Dome of the Rock" was
the Holy of Holies, as there is nothing to substantiate such an hypothésis.   Where, then, are
we to look for the site of the Temple, said to be
400 cubits or 600 feet square?   We find no difficulty in establishing one side at least of this square,
from which we may easily form the other three
sides.   Josephus says of the Temple, "The ground
was uneven, and like a precipice, and that great
pillars were raised to support the cloisters," etc.
This entirely agrees with the substructure of the
south-west of the platform; but what seems to
place the matter beyond doubt, the same author,
in a subsequent chapter, when referring to the
parley which took place between the Jewish leaders
and Titus, says, "Titus placed himself on the west
side of the outer court of the Temple, for there
was a gate on that side, and a *bridge that connected
the upper city with the Temple*," etc.   This bridge,
"which was in a line with the south porch of the
Temple," is undoubtedly that at Robinson's Arch,
to which I shall have occasion to refer hereafter,
as it crosses the valley and "leads to the upper
city."   In addition to this we have the evidence of
the Jews' "wailing-place" on the same side, and

situated within the 600 feet, where early tradition
would guide them, as Mr. Fergusson happily sug-
gests, to the point nearest' the Holy of Holies.
If, therefore, we take 600 feet from the south-
west corner northward, the "place of wailing"
would strike through the Holy of Holies, or centre
of the Temple; and take the square of this space,
the problem of the site of the Temple and its courts
is settled.

These passing remarks are simply the opinions I
have formed from my own reading and observation,
and may not be worth much in the estimation of
learned and scientific students. The reader will
therefore take them just for what he thinks them
worth. The subject is one which deserves the
fullest investigation.

After some time spent amidst these interesting
objects, we returned to the platform, and strolled
round the area of the Haram, inspecting the various
objects of architectural interest studded along its
surface. Some of these are of very pretty Saracenic
art, such as the marble cupola called the "Dome
of Solomon," the "Dome of Moses," and the gem
of them all, the "Dome of the Chair," or judgment
seat of King David. This graceful dome rests on
arches supported by light marble columns, which,

H

like those of the larger mosque, must have belonged
to an earlier Herodian or Roman temple.

We left the platform by the north-west gate at
which we entered, accompanied by our military
guide, and passed through the Moslem parts of the
town, along that depression which divides the ridges
of Aksa and Mount Zion, and ascended the latter to
the citadel, or Tower of David.   To the antiquarian
this is one of the most interesting remains of the
ancient city of David, and probably formed a stronghold of the Jebusite.   It also corresponds with
the situation of the Tower of Hippicus, of which
the reader will find a description in Book iv.
chap. 4, of Josephus's "Wars of the Jews."   This
building is on the western brow of Mount Zion,
overlooking the Valley of Hinnom.   The lower part
is early Jewish, built of those great bevelled stones
which we notice in the western wall of the Temple.
As the reader will often find these bevelled stones
referred to in describing Jewish architecture, I may
here explain that this "bevelling" resembles the
work in the panels of a door; about five inches of
the border of the stone all round is hewn smooth,
the centre projecting, sometimes rough and unhewn.
These stones are dovetailed, or joined together, with
lead or iron, so close that one can scarcely detect

the joints. This, I think, should be called Phœnician architecture: first, because we find it in some
of the Greek Islands, and on the coast of Syria,
where the Jews never had any footing; and further,
because the Jews had no taste for art, Solomon
employing the Phœnicians in the building of the
Temple, just as Herod availed himself of the arts
and artisans of Greece and Rome. But to return
to this ancient tower. The interior is now occupied
as a guard-room. We were conducted to the battlements, from which we had a magnificent view of
the city and country round. We parted here with
our courteous military guide, and proceeded northward, past the Jaffa Gate, and ascended the walls
leading round to the north of the city, till we got
near the Damascus Gate. From this point the
city is best seen in all its details; and with my
head filled with Josephus, I was able to form a
tolerably accurate idea of the outline he gives of
the city in his day, in the chapter to which I have
already referred. Although no city has undergone
such a change as ancient Zion, where valleys have
been filled up with *débris*, modern streets and houses
built fifty to sixty feet over accumulated rubbish,
still the four hills may be distinctly traced out—
that of Bezetha on the north-east, running south

and uniting with Mount Moriah, and terminating
in the low ridge of Ophel, and that of Akra on
the west, slightly descending towards the Pool of
Hezekiah, and joining Mount Zion on the south;
while the now slight depression, called by Josephus
the "Valley of the Cheesemongers," but better
known as the Tyropœon, divides Mount Zion from
Mount Moriah, and slopes down to the Pool of
Siloam.   This valley and the bridges over it, to
which I have already referred, and which united
the two hills or city of Zion with the Temple, I
shall have occasion to speak of in my researches
underground.   In the meantime I would direct the
attention of tourists to this spot, that they may
better understand, and be able to reconcile the
ancient with the present Jerusalem.

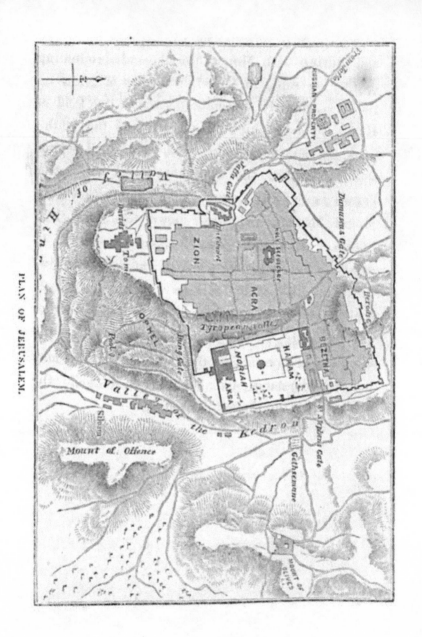

PLAN OF JERUSALEM.

56877

CHAPTER VII.

WE descended near to, and passed out at, the Damascus Gate, and turning a short way to the eastward, we came to what our guide called the Royal Caverns, but which are merely remains of a great subterranean quarry. They are one of the most remarkable sights in the city, yet I was surprised to find that many persons who had paid a passing visit to Jerusalem had never had their attention called to them. We crept, feet foremost, through a low arch in the rock, and with lighted candles proceeded down an incline over accumulating rubbish, which may be of any depth, till we came to the galleries and cutting of the quarry. Here were many of those great cyclopean stones still lying about, and round the sides are seen the deep incisions of the workmen's tools, fresh and sharp, just as if the men had left their work for a holiday. Proceeding onward, we came occasionally to a pool of water, and had to steer our way cautiously through the excavated galleries, till we had got well down to the lower part of the Bezetha ridge, when our guide would not proceed any farther with us. The materials taken from this quarry must have been immense, and most probably it was the chief source from which the walls and edifices were built. This finished our second day's journey.

On the third day, at 7.30 A.M., we visited the Church and Tomb of the Virgin, while the Greek and Armenian service was going on. This subterranean building is outside of St. Stephen's Gate, in the valley of the Kedron, and is in some respects a more interesting building than the Church of the Holy Sepulchre. The present entrance may be of the 11th or 12th century. The descent to the chapels is by a broad flight of sixty steps. The building is divided between the Greeks and Armenians, and the place was almost blocked up by pilgrims of both sects. The service was going on at both altars, the lights were dimmed with clouds of incense, and it was only after a little time that we could collect our ideas and see our way. We were taken charge of by one of the priests, and guided round to the back of the altar, where we were shown the tomb of the Virgin! as also that of the parents of the Virgin, Joachim and Anna! and of Joseph, the husband of Mary! It was not for me to inquire into these traditions. My Latin friend of the Holy Sepulchre would call it "Greek imposture;" but for the support of a corps of idle priests, one tradition is as good as any other. A little way to the right of this chapel, just at the commencement of the ascent of Mount Olivet, the Latin Church has inclosed a small space of ground of about an acre, including within the walls twelve or fourteen old olive-trees. This they call Gethsemane; and the Greeks, not to be behind their Latin brethren, have got their Gethsemane also, to the left, near the Chapel of the Virgin. Some matter-of-fact people have protested against there being two Gethsemanes, but I am inclined to think that both may be right, and that a considerable portion of the slopes of the mountain formed a public garden, as the name indicates, to which the citizens resorted, and where our Saviour and his apostles often retired after their labours and ministrations in the Temple, to the quiet sequestered walks, and vine and olive-clad terraces, beyond the noise and turmoil of the city.

We now ascended the Mount of Olives, by the middle road, to the mosque and minaret on the summit of the hill, within which is the so-called Church of the Ascension. We were permitted to

enter, and within a small cupola were shown a stone
with the footprints left by the Saviour on his ascension, which a priest and several pilgrims were devoutly
kissing. We ascended the dilapidated old minaret.
The view from this height has often been described,
but no pen can convey to the reader the feelings and
emotions that stir the heart on first viewing the
scenes around this sacred mountain. Here there is
no deceit or imposture : every object around passes
before the eye like the sight of familiar friends, all
doubts vanish, all our early lessons come back to us
with vivid reality, and a prayer of thankfulness rises
to our lips, that we have been privileged to survey
these sacred scenes. Looking to the east, over the
wilderness of Judea, the Dead Sea seems to be within
four or five miles of us, though the distance may be
twelve miles. A portion of the valley of the Jordan
may be traced, and beyond is the long line of the
mountains of Moab. I remember when some years
ago Holman Hunt exhibited his wonderful picture of
the "Scapegoat," many would-be critics pronounced
it a great exaggeration ; but if he took the view from
the spot where I stood, the scene could not have been
more true and faithful to the reality. The declining
sun lighted up with a perfect blaze the brown crags
and barren face of these mountains, and threw

dark shadows on their deep recesses. The view to the west embraced the whole city, which, as seen from this height, seemed to be transformed into a picture of unrivalled splendour. Every object, from the valley of the Kedron at our feet to the heights of Mount Zion, stood out in clear and bold relief, while the narrow dirty streets and abominations of the city were lost in shadows. What a scene this must have been when the magnificent Temple of Herod crowned the heights of Mount. Moriah, with towers and palaces, and all that wealth and art could devise !

Many writers on biblical history dispute the fact of this spot being the scene of the ascension : first, on the ground that our Saviour would not choose so prominent a place, seen from the whole city, for his ascension; and secondly, that St. Luke says, "He led them *out as far as to Bethany.* And it came to pass while he blessed them he was parted from them and carried up into heaven."

We descended the mountain by the eastern path, " which leadeth from Bethany," until we came to what are called the "Tombs of the Prophets," in the face of the hill which overlooks the Kedron. Our guide procured lights, and we crept in through a portion of these vaults, but could make little out of

JERUSALEM FROM THE MOUNT OF OLIVES

the place; and as we shall afterwards visit the
"Tombs of the Judges," and of the "Kings," to the
north of the city, I will not detain the reader here.
We then strolled down through the great Jewish
burying-ground, which stretches along the face of
the mountain, as far as the village of Silwan, or
Siloam. Towards this spot the Jews from all nations,
often in rags, poverty, and disease, drag their aged
limbs, that they may have a resting-place in the
valley of Jehoshaphat, near to the Temple of Zion.
The small white stones that mark these graves have
Hebrew inscriptions, as, for example, the following :—

"The tomb of the widow Malkah, relict of the
profoundly learned Rabbi Abraham Gatinaur,
author of 'Tirath Kepysh,' obit. on the 16th of
Shebit, 5523 (that is A.D. 1736)."

A number of others copied for me merely record
"the honoured worth" of some "Jacob" or "Abraham," with the age and date of demise.

In this valley are also the so-called Tombs of
Zacharias, Absalom, St. James, and Jehoshaphat.
The first of these is a monolith cut from the face of
the hill. Adjoining to this, and connected with it
by an excavated passage, is that of St. James, also
cut in the rock, and faced by a porch supported by

small Doric columns. That of Absalom resembles
the first in its base, but the upper part is built of
stone. From the village of Siloam we crossed the
valley to the Fountain of the Virgin, along the
ridge of Ophel, crossed the Tyropœon declivity, and
skirted the south wall to the southern brow of Mount
Zion, to visit the so-called Tomb of David, and the
Cœnaculum. We were led to the tomb through a
cowyard, ascended a broken-down outside stone
stair, and were taken to a dirty, neglected apartment, on one side of which was raised a kind of
cenotaph, covered with a piece of tattered green
cloth; we were told that "the real tomb of David
was in a cave below, which was now shut up." The
Church of the Cœnaculum, or Last Supper, is in the
hands of the Mohammedans, and forms a part of the
same building. A little beyond this is a building
called "the house of Caiaphas the high priest." We
now re-entered the city by the Zion Gate, and this
finished our third day's journey.

On the fourth day we again ascended Mount
Zion, to visit the church, convent, and college of
the Armenians. These, with their gardens, occupy
a large and prominent place on Mount Zion, round
which the Armenian inhabitants reside. The church
is a large and fine building, but its decorations are

of the most tawdry description, and its priests, determined not to be behind the Greek and Latin Churches, have introduced an amount of what may be irreverently called " stage property," with extraordinary legends, which, if they do not improve their piety, do great credit to their ingenuity and invention. Here we were shown a rough stone with an altar over it. I forget what sacred tradition was attached to it, but it had been stolen by the Latins, and was brought back from Rome by angels to its lawful possessors. In short, there seems to have been going on between these churches a system of petty larceny, aided by their respective angels, such as is quite shocking to ecclesiastical morality. Here John the Baptist was beheaded, and a round aperture in front of an altar, where the head of the saint is said to be buried, is devoutly kissed by the pilgrims. Not content with all these traditions, they have built into the side of an altar blocks of stones from the Jordan and Sea of Galilee, to which the pilgrims may pay their devotion, and money, and so save the trouble of going to these sacred localities.

On subsequent occasions I visited the Latin Convent and Church of St. John, which occupy a conspicuous site on the summit of Akra. This convent was the chief resort of travellers of all sects before the introduction of hotels, and they still avail themselves of its hospitality. Another Latin church, that of St. Anne, near St. Stephen's Gate, is worthy of a visit. It has lately been restored by the French Emperor, and is still under the hands of architect and artists.

Our fifth day we spent among the tombs outside the city. Proceeding out by the Damascus Gate, we first visited the "Tombs of the Kings," as they are now called, but which are referred to by Josephus as the "Monuments of Helena, Queen of Adiabene, near to which the third wall of the city extended." These are among the most extraordinary works round Jerusalem, and the amount of labour bestowed upon them is almost beyond conception. On the east side, facing the city, we enter a court of about 150 feet square. cut out of the solid rock. In front of this is a broad vestibule, with pillars, frieze, and projecting cornice, ornamented with fruits and flowers; and although these are very much defaced, there is still enough of character left to show that they belong to an early date, and may have had additions made to them in the Herodian period. Through this vestibule we descended into the tombs, consisting of a succession of chambers, in which are excavated, from the solid rock, a number of double

and single tombs, or loculi. Each of these chambers
had originally an ingenious stone door, fixed in a
groove, that shut so close as to appear like the native
rock. We had to creep on our hands and feet from
the one chamber to the other, till the scene became
so complicated that it was difficult to follow or
define the plan of the whole. Some of these
chambers contained as many as ten loculi, and
must have formed a royal receptacle for the dead,
the extent and labour of which it is scarcely
possible to conceive.

North-west from this point, along the ridge that
overlooks the valley of the Kedron, is a succession
of lesser tombs and caves, and we reach, at nearly
a mile distant, the Tombs of the Judges; but as I
return to these next day, under the able guidance
of the Rev. Dr. Barclay, I shall refer to them again,
and now go back to the plateau of rock and broken
ground lying between the northern wall of the city
and the Tomb of Helena. To what extent this
present bare plateau was included within the third
wall of Agrippa it is difficult to say. Josephus
speaks of the "Monuments of Helena" and the
"Sepulchral Caverns of the Kings" as distinct from
each other. The wall passed these caverns, and
stretched across to the heights over the Kedron,

turning southward till it joined the eastern wall
near the lower part of Bezetha. In this case the
third wall must have included the whole of the
intervening ridge; and this opinion is confirmed by
observing the numerous cisterns and broken aqueducts scattered about, indicating that the whole of
this space was covered at one time with streets,
villas, and gardens, the only vestiges of which now
left are the venerable olive-trees that seem to defy
all time and neglect. We returned by the Grotto
of Jeremiah, a large cave, partly natural and partly
excavated, in the face of the ridge, a little to the
north of the city wall. It is of immense size, and
leads into smaller caves, which we did not explore.
The front is enclosed by a wall, and the grotto is
in charge of a Haji, who demands one franc for
each person on entering. He has turned it into a
granary and stables for his cows and donkeys, and
the sight is scarcely worth the money. Another
walk round the eastern and southern wall to the
Zion Gate completed our fifth day's ramble.

On the sixth day I was invited by the Rev. Dr.
Barclay, of the Jewish Mission, to accompany him
to Neby Samwil, a mountain rising about four miles
north-west of Jerusalem, and crowned by a village
and mosque of that name. We left on horseback,

about noon, and rode out to the Tombs of the Judges, where we alighted, and taking candles with us, explored these rock-cut chambers as far as we could. The façade of these tombs is even more beautiful, and in better preservation, than that of the Tombs of the Kings; and the pillars, architraves, and ornamental tracery work give it the appearance of an early Roman temple. In the first chamber into which we entered we counted twenty-one loculi, in two tiers. We descended by a difficult passage to a lower chamber, in which we found eight of these loculi, and I was told by those who had more carefully examined these wonderful excavations, that there are about seventy of these receptacles for the dead. The whole face of this hill is studded with caves, partly natural, and excavated. We looked into a few of these, but they would have little interest for the reader after those I have attempted to describe.

From these tombs we rode along the face of a rugged hill, and over a part of the old Roman road, and ascended the hill which is crowned by the village and mosque of Neby Samwil.

The mosque stands about 600 feet over the plain of Gibeon. The building has all the marks of having been a Christian church, probably at the

I

time of the Crusaders. The transept and chancel,
though somewhat distorted by Moslem innovations,
can be distinctly traced. Attached to the south
end of the transept is the so-called Tomb of
Samuel. This is usually shut to Jew and Christian,
but a silver key, and a little quiet persuasion,
induced the attendant to admit us to this enclosure.
I expected to see some remains of Christian architecture, but found nothing but plain bare walls,
with a raised tomb in the centre, covered with a
coarse green cloth. The real tomb is said to be
in a vault below, but to that we could not get
access. Attached to the wing of the building is
a tall minaret, which we ascended, and the view
from which it is scarcely possible to describe. It
may be said to take in the whole physical aspect
of Palestine, and form a small epitome of biblical
history. This hill is not much higher than Mount
Olivet, but from its situation commands a more
extensive view of the country. With the aid of
a binocular glass we could see to the east distinct
objects along the mountains of Moab, and the
intervening wilderness of Judæa, and the domes
and minarets of Jerusalem; and on the west
trace the coast of the Mediterranean, and see the
vessels moving on its waters. To the south, the

view extended over Bethlehem, and the mountains that encompass Hebron; and to the north the hills of Galilee were seen vanishing into the blue ridge of Mount Carmel. I know no portion of the globe to be compared to this. It has a character entirely its own. As far as the eye can reach, it is one continued scene of rough and barren undulations, as if the waves of a mighty ocean had been arrested in their progress from north to south. From the local knowledge and studies of my companion, we were able to identify many objects, the names of which had been familiar to us from our earliest years. If the reader will turn to the tenth chapter of Joshua, he will find that in these fertile plains around Gibeon, and stretching "along the way that goeth up to Beth-horon," was fought that great battle which crowned with success the Jewish arms. Here Joshua defeated the assembled forces of the six petty sovereigns who then occupied the central ridges of Palestine, and laid the foundations of the Jewish Empire, from Mount Hermon to the borders of Edom. So many were the objects seen from this height, that it was with reluctance we again descended the tower.

We rambled through the little village, and ex-

amined the remains of some Jewish architecture,
which, judging from the cyclopean 'stones and
scarped rock on which they stand, must form the
remains of an ancient city. We then crossed the
plain, and ascended the " Hill of Gibeon," to the
small village which crowns its summit, now called
El' Jib. This is no doubt the site of the great
city of Gibeon, for " Gibeon was a great city, as
one of the royal cities, and all the men thereof
were mighty." This very pretty cone-shaped hill
rises terrace over terrace, like an artificial mound,
richly planted with vine and olive, and the valley
around it is in a higher state of cultivation than
any place I have seen near Jerusalem. A few
remains of the ancient city may still be traced
amidst the modern buildings, but not sufficient to
engage much time or attention. We rode quietly
back by the way we came. The day had been
very clear and fine, and now the sun was sinking
on the western horizon, and lighting up with
golden tints the mountain peaks, and towers, and
domes of the city, all tending to tranquillise the
mind, and raising in our hearts a prayer of gratitude for the pleasure and instructions of this happy
day's excursion. No pilgrim to Jerusalem should
omit this journey.

CHAPTER VIII.

HAVING now glanced at the principal objects of interest in and around the city, I was able to settle down quietly, and compare my own experience with my previous reading and impressions.

The modern Jerusalem, in its present aspect, may soon be dismissed. It is simply another type of Moslem decay and indifference. If we divide the city into four sections, we find that the portion lying immediately to the north-west of the Haram platform, probably the "lower city" of Josephus, is chiefly inhabited by the Turks and Arabs, with their dark, dirty, and unwholesome bazaars, narrow unpaved streets and alleys, such as may be seen in any Turkish town, and are neither picturesque nor inviting. South of this, on the slopes of Mount Zion, are the Jewish quarters, to which I shall have occasion to refer hereafter. The south-west of Mount Zion is called the Armenian quarter, and to the north of this, round the Jaffa Gate and Citadel, or Tower of David, are the church and residence of the Protestant bishop, and a number of the more respectable shops of the European and Jew proselytes. North, towards the Damascus Gate, are the two hotels, and the offices of the English, French, Prussian, and Austrian consulates. It is difficult to get a correct estimate of the population of Jerusalem; but the nearest approximation may be taken at 16,000, of whom the Jews form about one-third, or say 6,000; the Moslem, one-fourth, or 4,000; and the remaining 6,000 eastern and western Christians of various nations and sects. ·

The narrow winding streets and covered bazaars form such a complete labyrinth that it is difficult to find our way without a guide, until we master a few of the landmarks, and can take our bearings from place to place. These consist of two or three leading thoroughfares; that from the Jaffa Gate to the Haram, from west to east, and from the Damascus Gate on the north to the Armenian gardens on the south of Mount Zion.

If the reader will glance his eye over the map of Jerusalem, he will see that it occupies a ridge of mountain running from north to south, encompassed on the north and east by the valley of the Kedron, and on the west by the valley of Hinnom, which meet on the south below the Pool of Siloah.   This ridge is divided by a valley, now almost filled up, which runs down from the Damascus Gate, dividing Mount Zion from Mount Moriah and the Temple platform. The lower portion of this valley, dividing the upper city from the Temple, called the Tyropœon, is that to which I would direct attention, as it is here where the most interesting excavations are going forward. I presume most of my readers are familiar with the proceedings of the Palestine Exploration Society, the object of which is "the accurate and systematic investigation of the archæology, topography, etc., of the Holy Land, for biblical illustration;" and I trust that the honour and privilege of prosecuting this work to a successful end may be reserved for England and America, now peculiarly the "Lands of the Bible," and between whom there is no religious jealousy, but a willing and ready co-operation in all labours that tend to throw light around the sacred volume. This Society has been greatly aided in its efforts by its happy selection of men of great ability and industry to carry out its objects. The first expedition was conducted by Captain Wilson and Lieutenant Anderson, and the result of their surveys is now before the public. The second expedition is under the management of Lieutenant Warren, R.E., and a small staff of assistants. In carrying out the work it is necessary to exercise great tact, temper, and judgment, so as to meet the fanaticism and prejudices of the Moslems, and in this respect it would have been difficult to find in England a man more competent than Mr. Warren. These qualities have gained him such influence among all grades of the people, that I believe there is nothing now wanting but funds to carry on the discoveries successfully.

This is not the place to enter into details of the explorations, descriptions of which appear in the Reports sent to the subscribers to the Fund. I shall merely refer to some of the places which I visited with Lieutenant Warren, or his amiable assistant, Sergeant Birtles.

It may not be out of place, however, to direct the reader's attention to what has been said on the subject of the site of the Temple. The prevailing opinions of various writers may be classed under three heads : there are those who think that the Temple occupied the entire site of the present Haram platform ; those who place it in the centre over the "Dome of the Rock ; " and others, to whose view I confess I am a convert, believe it to have been at the south end, now occupied by the Mosque of Aksa. The first opinion I dismiss at once, as it is at variance with all the measurements given in the Bible, and by Josephus, and by the Rabbis. The second opinion would place the Temple on an elevated rock of some fifty or sixty feet, which could scarcely have been the threshing-floor of Ornan. We see outside of every village in Palestine at the present day a limestone plateau appropriated for this purpose, and may therefore reasonably suppose that the threshing-floor purchased by David from the Jebusite lay on the smooth slopes of the south ridge that overlooked the valley.

If we then dismiss the first two suppositions, what further evidence have we in support of the third hypothesis? First, as I have noticed before, we have the Jews' "wailing-place," indicating the wall of the Temple; secondly, the bridge or causeway referred to by Josephus, which crossed the deepest part of the valley to the upper city, in a line with the south porch of the Temple; and, lastly, there is no other place around Mount Moriah that tallies so well with the awe and surprise of the Queen of Sheba when she looked down from the courts of the Temple. We will suppose Solomon "in all his glory" descending from his palace in the upper city, to the deep valley—at that time perhaps spanned by a low bridge over the brook or aqueduct

—and ascending by a flight of steps and terraces to a height of nearly two hundred feet, to the courts of his magnificent Temple. "The king's ascent, by which he went up into the house of the Lord, and when she saw this there was no more spirit in her" (2 Chron. ix. 4).

CHAPTER IX.

I CONFESS I see great difficulties in reconciling my own crude notions with much that I have read and heard and the great uncertainty that hangs over every locality, the very names of which have been changed the one for the other. It will only be when we have full control over the Haram platform, and around it, that these doubts can be solved. When this much desired consummation may arrive, it is for politicians and nations to decide; but the day cannot be far distant.

We now know that the Tyropœon Valley was spanned by two if not more bridges. The lower one of these is now called Robinson's Arch, although I do not know why, as Dr. Edward Robinson only saw and spoke of that which was visible to every eye, viz., the remains of an arch springing from the western wall of the Haram. Near the south-west corner of the platform we notice a rough projection —this is the spring of the so-called Robinson's Arch.

It has been reserved for Lieutenant Warren to establish the fact that this was one of the bridges or causeways that crossed the Tyropœon Valley, and most probably that referred to by Josephus, where Titus held parley with the Jewish leaders, and which was "the passage from the outer court of the Temple to the upper city." Lieutenant Warren has sunk a shaft about forty feet from the wall, down which we descended by a succession of light rope ladders, till we got to the depth of fifty feet, where we found the *débris* or voussoirs of the fallen arch. Groping our way through these *débris*, we proceeded still lower, till we came to the pier and rock on which the arch rested. From this we lowered ourselves by rope, hand over hand, to a broken arch on which rested one of these large arch stones at a depth of eighty feet; and creeping through the small passage made by Lieutenant Warren's men, we discovered a canal or aqueduct running from north to south. On our return from this depth we crept, partly on all fours, through a gallery that has been run from the shaft to the foundations of the wall, and here we had the satisfaction of touching the scarped rock and foundations of the Temple wall. To one not accustomed to "sapping and mining" this exploration was no easy task, and certainly not to be

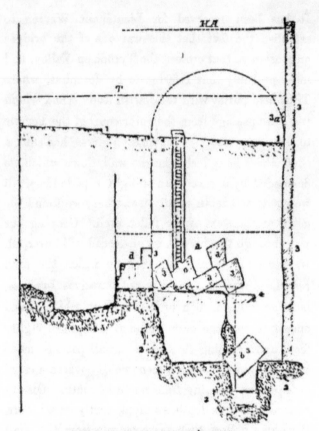

EXCAVATIONS AT ROBINSON'S ARCH.

1, Present surface of ground; 2, Rock; 3, Masonry; 3a, Spring of arch from Haram wall; 4, Pavement. *a*, Fallen voussoirs; *b*, Older voussoir; *d*, Pier *in situ*. A complete set of the photographs taken by the exploring party, with specimens of earthenware, glassware, and other relics, have been oh exhibition at the Egyptian Hall, London.

attempted by any one with weak nerves and delicate health.

On the next occasion we visited Wilson's Arch higher up the valley, and beyond the "wailing-place of the Jews." The first arch of this bridge, proceeding from the Haram wall, is, as far as I can judge, very similar to that of the lower bridge to which I have referred. Descending through the same description of *débris*, which consists of large masses of bevelled stones and broken voussoirs, forming the arch, we proceeded towards the west or opposite side of the valley, through an extraordinary number of complicated arched chambers and vaults, evidently of different periods, from the earliest Jewish to the Saracenic, leaving on my mind an impression that the first great arch in both bridges spanned the eastern and deepest part of the valley, and beyond these, as the valley rose, was a succession of smaller arches. To the north of these two bridges, where the valley ran round by Akra and was not so deep, there was one causeway or mound, if not two, communicating with what Josephus calls the suburbs, similar to that which connects the new and old town of Edinburgh.

The next day we descended two or three shafts that have been sunk near the south-east point of the

Haram wall. The first of these is about sixty feet deep, where we came to the scarped rock and foundation of the wall that encompassed Ophel; the depth of the other shafts decreased as we proceeded southward, till the last was only thirty feet below the surface. We have not been able to trace the further direction of this wall, but it is probable that it swept round the ridge, "bending above the fountain Siloam," as stated by Josephus, and that taking a westward direction, it joined the wall of the upper city near the present Armenian gardens. Farther south we came to the rock passage connecting the Fountain of the Virgin with the Pool of Siloam, which I did not enter. I mentioned before that a deep canal, or water-course, swept round the south-west corner of the Temple, at the deepest point of the Tyropœon Valley. It would look something like poetical inspiration, if this was

> " Siloa's brook that flowed
> Fast by the oracle of God,"

and leading down to the Pool of Siloam!

I shall very briefly refer to another of these excavations, not that it has any biblical or historical interest, but to show what labour, time, and expense the Jews bestowed on their fountains and aqueducts, and how highly they valued and extended the use of

these waters. At the junction of the valleys of
Kedron and Hinnom, some distance south of the
Pool of Siloam, there is a well, with open trough for
cattle, called "Joab's Well." Here Mr. Warren has
sunk a shaft, which we descended, and traced the
line of an aqueduct for 800 feet, covered with an
arched roof; and at intervals of sixty or eighty feet
there are flights of stairs cut in the rock, of considerable depth, descending from the face of the valley
to this aqueduct.

Those who have been in eastern countries will
understand and appreciate the necessity of water,
and the great merit attached to those who con-
tributed to its supply. The rajahs and rich baboos
of India, who bequeathed a sum of money to dig a
tank for the use of the village, were held in the
highest honour. In no part of the world could
this necessity of guarding against drought be more
necessary than in Jerusalem; and from the days of
Solomon to those of Hezekiah, the whole city must
have been intersected with conduits, pools, and
fountains. We learn that when the Assyrians
invaded Jerusalem, Hezekiah gave instructions to
stop the waters that supplied the fountains outside
the city, that when the enemy came "they might
not find much water;" and we find both in the

poetical and historical books of the Old and New
Testament constant allusions to these "fountains,"
"pools," and "waters." Every house had one or
more cisterns built or excavated within the court of
their house, for the preservation of rain water, as
may be seen, in a smaller degree, at the present day.
Many of these fountains and water-ways have disappeared. The great Fountain of Hezekiah, the
Pool of Bethesda, and the Pool of Gihon, are now
swamps or dry moats; hence, we hear of those
periodical visitations of famine and distress, when
the drought is prolonged, which call so strongly for
our aid and sympathy.

A movement was made some years ago to remedy
this want, by the introduction of a more regular
supply of water; and I was told that a benevolent
lady, whose sympathising heart and open hand is
ever ready to succour and assist the distressed, came
forward with the offer of a large contribution for this
object, and I believe plans were made and operations
commenced, when the agents of the "sick man"
stopped the work on some fanatical plea or other;
and so Jerusalem, like every other part of the
Turkish empire, is now without its "living waters,"
in every sense of the expression.

Amongst the doubtful localities of scriptural ob-

K

jects may be mentioned the present Bethesda.   This
does not answer the description of the pool where
" the water was troubled," which more likely belonged to some branch of the water of Siloam,
whereas this was evidently one of the great reservoirs for the supply of the Temple or lower city.
It occupies a space of 300 feet against the north-
east wall of the Haram.   While I was at Jerusalem
Captain Warren sunk a shaft about 20 feet out from
the north wall of the Haram, and after considerable
trouble on account of water, succeeded in reaching
a bottom of firm concrete, as if intended for a
reservoir; and carrying a short gallery on to the
wall, he found a lining of stone and plaster.   The
pool is 80 feet deep, but has now about 40 feet of
accumulated rubbish.

Some writers contend that the Temple and
Tower of Antonia covered the whole space of the
present platform, and have conjectured that this
so-called pool was simply a moat for the protection
of the tower; but apart from the absurdity that the
Temple and courts occupied anything like this great
space, the late researches and excavations have com-
pletely exploded this hypothesis; and whether
this be the "Pool of Bethesda" of Scripture or
not, it was unquestionably a great reservoir sup-

plied by rain, and perhaps communicating with springs.

The other excavations that we visited are not perhaps of sufficient interest to the reader, I will therefore conclude with a few remarks on "the walls and gates of Jerusalem," which are so often referred to in sacred history. The circle of the present walls is about two and a half miles. The direction of the ancient walls, first, second, and third, is involved in doubt and uncertainty; but there are certain landmarks that cannot be mistaken. We know that the first wall encompassed Mount Zion, and joined the south and north wall of the Temple, on Mount Moriah. The second wall, though a mere offshoot of the first, is the one which involves the greatest amount of controversy, for on its direction depends the authenticity or otherwise of the site of the Church of the Sepulchre being on the real Calvary, and "garden where the body of our Saviour was laid." I have read a great deal on this subject, from Josephus down to the latest controversy, and I cannot help coming to the conclusion that the second wall went round the entire hill of Akra, and consequently included the site of the present church, with all its traditions, and that the real Golgotha and sepulchre were to the north of the Temple. This second wall, as I have stated, made the circle of Akra and the "lower city," joining the Temple Area at the Tower of Antonia. The third wall extended from near the present Jaffa Gate, north by the Damascus Gate, including the hill or rising ground of Bezetha, from which point the Romans attacked the city, and made their way to the second wall. "There were certain parts of the city," Josephus says, "that were encompassed with impassable valleys, where there was only one wall." This would, of course, apply to the east and west, overlooking the Kedron and Hinnom, on the line of the present walls. I have already referred to the wall that "encompassed Ophel," part of which we explored, and where Lieutenant Warren has since discovered some foundation-stones with cut and painted characters left by the Phœnician builders.

I have spoken of Mount Zion in preceding chapters, as it is understood on the present maps; but the real position of Mount Zion is, like many other places in and around Jerusalem, involved in uncertainty. I will not presume to enter into controversy with the learned scholars and topographers who have discussed, and settled, to their own satisfaction, the sites of the various places referred to in

biblical history; but simply state, that I am inclined to follow those who believe the hill now
called Akra to be Mount Zion, "the City of David,"
and that the upper city, or "market-place," was
Jebus, or Jerusalem, in contradistinction to the
Akra, or stronghold of David; and that in after
years, when, by war and destruction, many of the
landmarks were destroyed, and the height of the
northern hill reduced to fill up the valley, and
bring the lower city to a level with the Temple, the
whole space, including the Temple, came to be
designated "the Zion, the holy city of David." No
doubt the south hill was afterwards taken possession of by King David, and there he may have
erected a citadel, and palaces and other great
buildings rose around it, from the time of David
to Herod; and this may partly account for the
early Christians identifying this hill with Mount
Zion.

Curiously enough, Josephus does not once, to my
knowledge, use the term Mount Zion; but distinctly
speaks of the upper city as distinct from the lower
city, and "City of David." In the fifth book and
fifth chapter of the "Wars of the Jews," he says:
"The city was built upon two hills, which are
opposite to one another, and have a valley (the

Tyropœon) dividing them, at which the corresponding rows of houses on both hills ended. Of these hills, that which contained the upper city was much the higher, and in length more straight. . . The other hill, which was called Akra (the citadel), and sustains the lower city, is crescent-shaped. Over against this was a third hill (Mount Moriah), by nature lower than Akra, and formerly separated by another broad valley. But afterwards, in the times when the Maccabees ruled, they filled up the valley with earth, desiring to connect the city with the Temple; and working down to the height of Akra, they made it lower, so that the Temple might appear above it."

It will thus be seen that the north hill, now called Akra, was that connected with the Temple by the "lower city," and the whole embraced both the poetical and historical expressions of "Mount Zion," "the Holy Mount," "the City of the Lord," "the Zion of the Holy One of Israel."

If we cannot distinctly trace the line of the first two walls from the accounts I have referred to, one thing is perfectly certain, that the upper city, as well as Akra and the lower city, were included within the walls, and that the site of the present "Church of the Sepulchre" must have been in

THE GOLDEN GATE.

the very centre of the city at the time of the
Crucifixion.

There are at present five gates or entrances into
the city, viz., the Jaffa Gate to the west, the
Damascus Gate to the north, St. Stephen's Gate to
the east, an obscure gate in the Tyropœon Valley,
called the Dung Gate, and the Zion Gate at the
south-west corner of the city. These gates, though
chiefly Saracenic, are on the site of the ancient
walls. Two gates are built up, one called the Gate
of Herod, the other the Golden Gate. Our engraving is from an excellent photograph of the
latter from the inside, by Mr. Bergheim, banker,
of Jerusalem. It will be observed that the architecture is of pure, or rather impure, Corinthian
order, for Mr. Fergusson does not admit of its being
of the best Roman period, but of the time of the
Emperor Constantine. There is no doubt, however,
that it is of the date between that of Constantine
and Justinian; and if erected by the former, it may
have been the eastern entrance to that Basilica
which Mr. Fergusson assigns to the first Christian
emperor. This gate has been walled up by the
Mohammedans, in consequence, it is said, of a
tradition that by this gate Christian conquerors of
the city would enter. Outside of this gate there is

a Mohammedan burying-ground, which renders it difficult to obtain permission to make excavations here; but Lieutenant Warren has lately sunk a shaft about 140 feet to the south-east of the gate, and run a gallery over the rock and *débris*, with considerable labour and risk of life; and forty feet from the present gate he has come against a massive wall, running north and south, which is yet unaccounted for.

One regrets that so many of these partial discoveries are comparatively lost, as the shafts have to be immediately filled up again; but no satisfactory conclusions that will link together can be reached till the people who have no business there are turned aside out of the way.

CHAPTER X.

I HAVE only casually referred to the Wailing-place. Here the Jews assemble every Friday afternoon from 2 P.M. to sunset. It is a portion of the ancient Temple wall, standing about half-way between the two bridges that I have referred to, constituting perhaps the oldest and best remains. Some of the stones are twenty-five feet long by five feet deep, the bevelling still distinct. The wailers I saw were chiefly old Polish Jews, of both sexes: some were reading psalms, others praying and thrusting their heads into the crevices of the wall; others I noticed pushing pieces of paper into the cavities that divide the stones, and which my companion informed me were petitions from distant Jews, who, he added, were too wise to come themselves. I did not at that time see any of these things in a ridiculous light, but was rather stirred with sorrow and sympathy for these aged pilgrims, weeping like broken-hearted children, the big tears flowing down their sad and

care-worn cheeks—the earnest appeal to the God
of their fathers for the restoration of their Zion.
The sight was heartrending, and I am not ashamed
to confess that I felt a moisture in my eyes at the
sight of so much apparent misery. One may feel
grieved at their blind and stiff-necked rejection of
their Messiah and "the new covenant," but the
heart is wrung with pity at their unhappy lot. I
felt so much overpowered by the influences of
this extraordinary scene, that I could have remained till its close, but was reminded by my
companion that we were engaged to attend the
weekly prayer-meeting of the Protestant Mission
and Jewish proselytes. I refer to this engagement
simply to show the contrast between these children
of joyful hope, and those who seemed to be in
hopeless despair.

This meeting was a happy gathering of the
children of Israel who had sought and found their
Redeemer and Comforter. Bishop Gobat and his
family were there, and the other clerical members
of the mission. Among the laity present the foremost man in Jerusalem for devotion to his profession and unbounded philanthropy, was Dr. Chaplin,
who has charge of the hospital for the relief
of sick Jews, and I can speak with confidence of

the unsectarian spirit and broad Christian principles on which this relief is carried out. The
piety and truly Christian character of this gentleman is so well known to all classes in Jerusalem,
that I should only give pain to his generous and
sensitive feelings, if I were to make any mention
here of the many grateful expressions I heard
of his unflagging labours as physician of both
body and soul. I cannot here refrain from men-
tioning the name of Miss Dickson, who has charge
of the girls' school for the education of the children of Hebrew parents, as well as the industrial
school, where Jewish women are taught needle-
work, and paid for their labours. There were also
present the Revs. Dr. Barclay, Mr. Bailey, and
Mr. Frankel, and families, all equally zealous in
the good work, and whose example and walk of
life go beyond all precept with those amongst
whom they labour. The meetings are conducted
with prayer and discussions, and are both profitable
and instructive.

In addition, the Jewish proselytes have their own
weekly meetings, and these afforded me as great a
pleasure as anything I met with in Jerusalem. In
"an upper chamber," just such a one as the brethren
may have met in when their Lord appeared to them,

were assembled some thirty Jewish proselytes, quiet, respectable, unassuming men. After an opening prayer, a chapter was read, and then each verse was discussed by all who chose to offer an opinion, and I confess I was very much surprised to find them all so well acquainted with the Scriptures, and so able to expound their meaning. It may not be out of place here to remark, that nothing can be more unjust than the opinion, too general, I fear, among both Jews and Christians, that there is no sincerity in these conversions. I do not believe that I ever met with more honest and sincere men. Their convictions seemed deeply rooted, and their conduct and conversation in other relations of life convince me that there is a good field of labour here, and that it is yielding its fruits.

There could scarcely be, in this world, a greater contrast than between these men and their miserable and unhappy countrymen to whom I have already referred. I was invited to accompany a dispenser of charity among the distressed Jews, and learned that out of nearly 8,000 Hebrews in Jerusalem, half are living on charity, chiefly supplied, I believe, by the wealthy Jews of Europe. Those readers who have strolled through the Ghetto, the Jewish quarters of Rome, or through that portion

of the city of Prague inhabited by the Jews, will
remember the foul and miserable condition in which
"the peoples" appeared to live there; but even in
this misery there was life and industry. In the
Jewish quarters of Jerusalem, on the south-east
slopes of the present Mount Zion and the Tyropœon
Valley, the picture of dirt, and sickly squalor, and
perfect indolence, surpasses anything I have ever
yet seen. The houses are generally inclosed in a
small court, through which you have to pick your
way over all manner of abominations. I was shown
into two or three of the dark cells in which they
live. I could not at first see any one through the
smoke. At length I observed three sickly-looking
men and some children lying on ragged quilts, and
an old woman cooking something in the middle of
the floor. As soon as our mission was known, their
complaints and pleadings were most distressing. I
naturally inquired how these people managed to
exist without occupations, and how it happened that
the wealthy Jews of Europe permitted the existence
of such distress among their co-religionists, and was
told that they did in various ways make large con-
tributions for their relief, but that it only en-
couraged a greater number to resort to "Zion"
under the pretence of religious zeal, and that of

the money sent one-half is taken by the rabbis, who read and expound the Talmud, and only half reserved for the people. There is, behind this, something far more serious and injurious to the character of these foreign Jews than their indolence and mendicity, and which I think ought to be taken into consideration by the various European governments whose protection they claim.

I have seen a good deal of Mohammedan, Hindoo, and Buddhist life, and I doubt if there is anything in their habit of life more degrading and immoral than among these foreign Jews. One of their rabbis, a man perhaps of fifty, but so dirty and grizzled that it was difficult to tell his age, took us into a small upper room and showed us thirty-eight volumes of the Talmud, which I understood he read to the people. As we were coming out, my companion, a most benevolent lady, took some notice of a pleasant little girl, about thirteen or fourteen years of age, who was knitting at the door. "This girl," my companion said, "is the wife of that rabbi, who pretends to instruct the people—perhaps his fourth or fifth wife; and when he is tired of her, he has only to assign some frivolous reason, and on the payment of a trifling sum the chief rabbi dissolves the marriage. We have some five or six of these young divorced wives from fourteen to sixteen years of age now in the industrial school." If these idle, worthless men claim the protection of the different European governments to which they profess to belong, we naturally ask why they are allowed to set at nought the authorities of these countries by violating all the laws of civilisation. Since my return to Europe I have referred to this subject, in conversation with several rabbis and influential laymen, and pointed out what I witnessed of the moral and physical degradation of their co-religionists in Jerusalem. They one and all repudiated them as " idle and ungrateful vagabonds."

A Hebrew gentleman, well known for literary ability and kindly disposition, said to me, with some warmth, "If I had any influence with the governments, I would have every one of these 3,000 or 4,000 idle Jews turned out of Jerusalem, to find useful occupation elsewhere, *and earn their bread by the sweat of their brow.*" We were agreed on their state of degradation, but we saw the cause from a very different point of view. The "light" which they have rejected might have cleared up some of these difficulties. These men have been taught to believe that this chastisement is a sort of honour which is left for them especially to sustain,—that for

others it is a privilege to contribute to their main-
tenance; and that on the coming of their Messiah
their temporal kingdom will be restored, "when
kings and queens will think themselves honoured by
being raised of God, in serving them, and the
Gentiles should lick up the dust of their feet."

There are some excellent Christian divines, for
whom I have great personal respect, who have devoted much time and study to Bible prophecies, and
have attempted to interpret them to meet their own
particular views with little profit.

We had a quiet kindly gentleman living with us
at the hotel; no one could learn what had brought
him to Jerusalem. When he was asked if he had
seen such and such things, his reply was that "he
had not come to Palestine for sight-seeing, but for
higher purposes." As he was a countryman of mine
I was appealed to, to know what had induced the
poor old gentleman to come so far from home; and
drawing him into an argument, I found that his
weakness was "the approaching restoration of the
Jews to their temporal kingdom!" I endeavoured
to persuade him that he was taking too close an
interpretation, and that it was the kingdom of Christ
that was to be restored to Zion, in which all nations
would be partakers; that the Jews, as Jews, might

L

never again become a temporal power in Palestine; and that without any violation of Scriptural prophecy. His feelings were still further shocked, and I fear his faith slightly shaken, when he was told by a much respected Jewish proselyte, that "there were very few Jews of education, wealth, or influence in Europe, from the rich banker to the pawnbroker, who either expected or wished for a Jewish kingdom, and that they preferred the protection of English, French, or German governments to any of their own countrymen or co-religionists."

Apropos of this subject, while I was revising my journal I had a letter from a friend in Berlin, in which he informed me that the reformed Jews and rabbis of Germany had held a synod, in which the subject of omitting from their ritual the allusion to the "Restoration" was considered, and the omission was regarded by a large majority as most desirable. It may be interesting to the reader if we quote the opinions of some of the speakers. A learned rabbi says: "The religion of Judaism is one of truth and enlightenment; that the people of Israel have retained and will retain the mission of being the exponents of this doctrine, which will become the common property of the entire enlightened world; and that Israel *will expand into mankind.*

All expressions limiting or disturbing this exalted view are improper. All relative to a revival of Israel's nationality must therefore be removed, and the distinction between Israel and other nations, as existing in former ages, should not be noticed in the prayers. On the contrary, satisfaction should be expressed on account of the continual decrease of ancient restrictions. Nor should the delight of this noble spiritual calling degenerate into the appearance of arrogance or inuendos touching other nations. The anticipations of the future must be such as to awaken the joyous hope that the human race will be united in truth, justice, and peace. The belief in the restoration of a Jewish state in Palestine, and the rebuilding of the Temple, as the centralising spot of Israel and gathering of the scattered people—in fact, all that is connected with the restoration of bygone times and circumstances, has entirely departed from the range of our expectations ; and the expression of the realisation of such hopes should be expunged from our prayers."

These opinions will no doubt be indignantly repudiated by many of the good old orthodox Jews ; but they look very much like a stepping-stone to our idea of universal Christianity, and are not a bad answer to those who rack their brains to interpret the pro-

phecies. It is not my intention, however, to touch
on controverted points respecting the " restoration
of the Jews to their ancient kingdom." I simply
feel it a duty to give this testimony of what I saw
and heard of their present state, and that but very
slightly, as I have in my possession documents to
substantiate much beyond what I have stated.

I may, with perfect truth, say that I have no
personal feeling on this matter, except that of sorrow
for the present condition of these unhappy exiles.
I have been a humble advocate for national and
individual emancipation ever since I was able to
take an interest in human progress, and would not
willingly give offence to either political or religious
aspirations, least of all to the people who were the
divinely-appointed guardians of our faith, among
heathen nations, for many ages ; through whom
we have received " the law and the prophets," and
of whom were the apostles; and nothing in history
has shocked me more than the remorseless animosity
with which the Roman Church has persecuted the
Jewish people,

CHAPTER XI.

BEFORE I bid adieu to Jerusalem, it is proper that I should refer to our own and the Prussian Protestant missions and missionaries in and near the city, among whom I spent some of the most happy and intellectual days of my sojourn here, the recollection of which will be a source of pleasure and comfort to me as long as I live. Beginning from the outside, as we approach the city from the west, the first object that attracts our attention to the left is the orphan asylum, a plain, unpretending building, established, I think, by Mr. Schneller, chiefly for the orphans of the Damascus massacre. There are about fifty boys here, Greeks and others, provided with a comfortable home, and receiving a good moral education, who are instructed in useful trades, by which they will be able to make a respectable living. Those who show superior talents are better, or rather further instructed, and prepared for missionary work and teaching among their own

people. It gladdens one's heart to see these boys
so cheerful, and happy, and good, who, had they
been left to their misfortunes, might have been
grovelling in darkness, if not in crime.

Nearer to the city on the right is the newly-built
institution of the Prussian Deaconesses. The reader
may remember my reference to the large establishment of these excellent ladies in Smyrna. This is
conducted on much the same principle, and is a
perfect model of cleanly, thrifty, and healthy life
and activity. Everything is done under their management, and they are now bringing earth, and preparing gardens in which the pupils may be occupied.
These girls, Greek and Arab, will take a large
amount of useful information and a high moral
tone into the world with them, and as wives, and
mothers, and teachers, will do a vast deal more good
than all the dreamers on the restoration of a Jewish
kingdom.   .

We are now going to pay our last visit to our
friends on Mount Zion. On the north-west of the
ridge, overlooking the Citadel and Tower of David,
an open space has been cleared away, and on it
stands the Protestant cathedral, or consulate church,
and adjoining it the residence of Dr. Gobat, Anglo-
Prussian Bishop of Jerusalem, as also the residence

of the Rev. Dr. Barclay, the missionary and pastor of the church.

. It was my privilege to be in Jerusalem and to worship on Mount Zion with my Protestant brethren for four consecutive Sundays. On the last Sunday I stood sponsor, with a great traveller, whose friendship I highly value, and who was as old and grey as myself, to the child of a Jewish proselyte, whose good character I had become acquainted with. This last Sunday bears strongly on my recollection. I do not know if it was nervous weakness or the solemnity of the place and occasion, but when I returned from the font I was glad to relieve my oppression by giving licence to a few tears. I had also to pay my last visit to the bishop's school or orphanage on the south spur of Mount Zion, outside the wall, and overlooking the Valley of Hinnom. This school has been established, and I believe chiefly supported, by Dr. Gobat. Here are some fifty boys, of all nations, colours, and parentage, and among them a few of the Damascus victims. I occasionally addressed these boys, and I found them very cheerful and intelligent, and radiant with affection and gratitude to those good and self-denying men who were labouring for their future welfare and happiness.

I should refer to the labours of Dr. Gobat's wife and daughters and Miss Dickson among the Jewish and Arab children, and in the Industrial Institution; but I can do but small justice to their active labours, and can only pray that they may be supported with spiritual and temporal means to carry on their good work.

It may not be out of place here to offer a few words of assurance and comfort to those who contemplate making this pilgrimage, and have any misgivings as to the reception they may meet with in this city. Besides the Latin and Greek Hospices and private accommodation, there are two hotels, the "Damascus" and "Mediterranean," both kept by Germans, civil and attentive men, who are most anxious to promote the comfort of their guests, and to assist them in every way. The charge for board and lodging, with the use of a public sitting-room, is twelve to fourteen francs per day. The table supply is equal to the average hotels of Europe, and as a rule, tourists will find desirable society, and men of travelled experience and extensive information.

A great deal has been said about the prudence of bringing English saddles, bridles, and other necessary articles for travelling in the East, on account of the badness of native riding gear.   I

have had a good deal of experience on horseback,
and I confess I never rode more comfortably than
I did on this journey, on the common Oriental
saddle. The bits are certainly ugly-looking and
forbidding articles to the eye of an English horse-
man, and seem severe and irritating to the animal's
mouth; but if the rider is content with four or
five miles an hour, over limestone crags and
boulders, and will let the bit lie easy in the horses'
mouths, these docile animals will carry him safely
any distance, and with much more comfort than
one is led to expect. The chief thing is to see
that the gear is sound and strong, or make the
muleteer change the girths and stirrups if necessary.

I had waited some days longer than I intended
in Jerusalem, with the view of joining, from objects
of economy as well as comfort, two American
gentlemen, a clergyman and his deacon, who were
proceeding northward. It must be understood that
the expense of dragoman, cook, muleteer, etc., is
nearly as much for one as for three or four. A
single person could not travel in this manner under
£3 or £3 10s. per day, whereas we three were
able to carry out our journey at the rate of £3 15s.
per day. Mustaffa, a young athletic Mussulman,

recommended by the American consul, undertook
the duty of dragoman, to supply cook, muleteer,
mules, etc., and to provide us with food, tents,
guides, and pay all necessary expenses. The
American gentlemen selected their horses with
great care. I had not left myself time to attend
to this matter, and took what the muleteer
brought me—a rough-looking, half-Arab horse.
I merely saw that his knees and back were sound;
and, as it happened, he turned out the best horse
on our journey. We had in all four horses and
five mules, two tents, cooking apparatus, with all
necessary provisions for ten or twelve days'
journey, an excellent cook, and muleteer and two
assistants. I took an agreement on my own part,
and had it registered at the office of the British
consul. My American friends took no agreement,
and fortunately had no occasion to regret their confidence. It is as well, however, to have an agreement registered at the office of our own consul in
case of illness or loss of property.

CHAPTER XII.

It was arranged that we should start at 8 A.M. on the 11th December, but as my travelling companions had a good deal of luggage which required to pass the custom-house, we did not get off till 10 A.M. I should wish to blot out of my journal the records of the next three days of our journey, as they are only a recital of personal troubles and suffering, were it not that my experience may be useful to future travellers. The morning looked very gloomy when we started, and we had just got a mile beyond the Damascus Gate when the black clouds that had been coming up from the south burst upon us with all the violence of a tropical storm, of rain and hail, and heavy gusts of wind. I attempted to put up my light silk umbrella, but before I could get it open it was blown into tatters. Now I found out my mistake in not having a properly made macintosh waterproof dress. My companions had furnished themselves in Edinburgh with a complete suit of india-rubber from head to foot. I had only

an india-rubber sheet wrapped round me, which I
found very inconvenient in riding, as one ought to
have the hands and legs in perfect freedom.   These
storms, which continue for days, are the chief objects to guard against in providing travelling costume.   A small portmanteau may carry all that is
required for a two months' journey in Palestine,
but the india-rubber suit is indispensable.   Go-
loshes, leggings, overcoat, and cap, with lappet to
come over the neck, a sheet, or one or two pieces of
india-rubber cloth, very stout, should be taken to
wrap round portmanteau, or other luggage, from
the want of which we had our linen and books
damaged.

It may be as well to mention here that the best
time to travel in Palestine is in autumn and spring.
In October and November one may escape these
storms.   In December and January they are certain,
and run into March, when they are sometimes
severe, so that one should always be prepared for
them.

But to return to our journey.   The rain fell in
torrents, and when we got to the summit of Scopus,
the last ridge that overlooks the Holy City, we were
just able to turn our horses' heads to the storm, and
take a last look at its domes and walls.   We had

little opportunity for sentiment, or quiet contemplation; but who can ever forget Jerusalem?

We left the scenes which I have described, with the Hill of Gibeon on our left, passed by Ramah, and soon after mid-day arrived at Bireh, the Beeroth of Scripture. Here we took shelter in the ruins of an ancient mosque, and under its broken dome spread our carpet and had our lunch, after which we rode round to see the ruins of an old Gothic church built by the Knights Templars. It is still a very interesting ruin, but what will recall the name of this place to the Bible reader is its being one of the four cities inhabited by the Gibeonites when they made their wily league with Joshua.

We now struck off a little to the right, and at 4 P.M. reached Bethel. This was the first night of my experience in an Arab house. The wind was too high and the rain too heavy to admit of pitching our tents, and we found shelter in one of the few stone buildings in the village. This was a square vault arched over. The centre was occupied by the cattle. At the back was a raised granary, with places for the fowls to roost, and on one side, under the arch, which was leaking all over, was a raised platform where the village sheik and his family resided.

Our dragoman made terms with them that they should turn out the cattle, and find shelter for themselves, leaving the platform to us. Mustaffa was master of the occasion, and showed all his resources; got out candles, for there was no light except through the small aperture by which we entered. The cook set to work below us, and while they were laying out our beds and getting dinner ready, we remounted and rode round the ruins of the ancient city. Amongst these are the remains of an old Greek church, now covered with rubbish, but by creeping through the ruins we found portions of columns, and could trace out the form of the church. Scattered over the plateau of the ridge on which the village stands, there are still the *débris* of old Jewish architecture, and a cistern of nearly 300 feet square, which is clearly of ancient Jewish construction. Nothing but a sense of duty and a strong desire to see as much as possible of this place, associated with the earliest history of the Jewish people, would have tempted us then to explore these ruins under such unfavourable circumstances.

Our cook had prepared a good dinner for us, and as the rain increased, and the thunder rolled over our dark vault, we were half inclined to congratulate ourselves that we were under shelter, dirty and miserable as it was. We lighted a brushwood fire, but the smoke got into our eyes; we tried to read, but found this impossible, and in self-defence turned into our beds. After a time our lights went out, and I then began to realise the density of the darkness, and the dismal scene around. The fatigues of the day began to tell upon me, and I felt inclined to dress and rush out into the storm which was still raging; and how glad I was when I heard the cocks crowing, and saw the first dawn of light struggling through the small door! Mustaffa was soon in activity, and the old cook quickly got up a capital breakfast. The storm was still raging, and our muleteer began to show symptoms of mutiny and reluctance to pack up. Mustaffa was called to account. The reply was that we should remain here for the day, that tents and baggage were saturated with the excessive rain, and the roads would be impassable in certain parts. To me it was simply a choice between being smoked and choked, or being drowned, and I preferred the latter alternative, and we all agreed that we should start; and with some scolding and loss of time we got off by 10 A.M.

It was our intention when we started from Jerusalem to make a journey of two days only to

Nabulus, but the very severe weather and state
of the roads, or rather the absence of all roads,
interfered with this arrangement, and we resolved
to stop the second night at Shiloh, but by some
blunder or misunderstanding our muleteer pushed
on to Nabulus, and left us helpless. The day
proved worse than the previous one. The wind
and rain were still heavy, and every passage flooded.
Soon after leaving Bethel we came to an ascent
leading through a deep gorge of the mountain,
which was now swollen with a rapid torrent. The
horses toiled up to the girths, slipping and flounder-
ing over the sharp rugged precipice, till my companions got uneasy, dismounted and led their
horses, picking their way along the rugged face
of the ravine, over their knees in water. I had
by this time gained complete confidence in my little
horse, and was prepared to stick on his back
wherever he would carry me. I gave him the
reins, and he toiled on, sometimes actually pulling
himself up by his forefeet till he got a fresh hold
on the slippery limestone rock. We had not long
surmounted this difficulty when we came to a
swamp partly covered with water, and saturated
to the depth of three or four feet. Here our
mules broke down, and their burdens of beds,

portmanteaus, etc., were lying in the mud. We
remained on the borders of the swamp till we
saw the animals recovered and reloaded, and then
followed them with great difficulty, scarcely ex-
pecting that our horses would struggle through it.

We now saw before us the hill on which Shiloh
stands, but between us and the ancient city, where
the Ark was first planted in Canaan, "there was a
deep gulf." A river lay at the base of the mountain, so swollen by the late rains, that we had great
doubts of getting across. Mustaffa, after taking a
survey of the river up and down, spurred his horse
over the soft bank into the rapid stream. The
animal lost its footing and almost disappeared.
Mustaffa stuck to the saddle and got across with
a good ducking. I was immediately behind him;
and seeing no alternative but to follow, I plunged
in, keeping my horse's head up the stream. My
good little horse struggled across, with the water
up to the saddle, and carried me safely over. I
called on my friends to follow, but they made no
movement; I then rode after our dragoman, who
I found had gone in search of a fellah or shepherd
to learn if there was any other safer ford. On
returning we met our friends, who had taken
courage from despair, and crossed the river a little

M

higher, with less damage than ourselves. We arrived at Shiloh wet and weary about 5 P.M. Mustaffa again procured us shelter in a miserable vault. I thought that our previous night's lodging was about the most wretched that any human being could occupy, but "in every depth there is a deeper still." At Bethel they took out the cattle, and found quarters for themselves, leaving us the stable and platform, but on this night our own horses and their cattle occupied the lower part, and we had to take our places on the raised platform with the family, consisting of three men, an old woman, and a little girl, the latter doing all the work while the men were smoking their pipes. I mentioned before that our mules and baggage had gone on, so that we had neither candles, charcoal, nor provisions. Their small oil cruse served only to make the dark more dismal. The vault was in every respect similar to that of the previous night, except that it was darker and dirtier. The encrustations of smoke seemed the accumulation of years.

It was time to think of our wet clothes. Some light brushwood was got from outside, and a fire kindled. The smoke could not escape, and soon filled our dungeon. There was no help for it but to dry our stockings at this fitful flame, as we had

nothing dry to put on in the morning. Two or
three neighbours had stepped in to stare at us, and
gossip over the poor demented travellers helplessly
wandering over a country in which they were
strangers. When we proposed to retire the old
sheik brought out two suspicious-looking quilts, one
of which we placed below us, and we made a covering of the other. The visitors having finished
their pipes and their observations, the family prepared to retire. The old woman squatted down
alongside the clergyman, the sheik between her
and the little girl, and the two others beyond them
managed just as they could. The embers of the fire
were now sinking, the dim lamp had gone out, and
the darkness seemed intense; the thunder, the
howling wind, and the pelting rain could be heard
through the little aperture in the wall; the hard-
boiled eggs and half-baked Arab scones "sat like a
demon on my chest." I could get no rest, and it
was frequently a question with me whether I should
go out and face the storm or remain in this dungeon
to be stifled. This state of things was occasionally
relieved by the quarrels of the horses and donkeys,
and the remonstrances of their keepers. Towards
morning the rain abated a little, and as we had
no packing to do we got on horseback soon after

daylight, and rode round the village, but saw very little of interest. There are the ruins of an old church of the time of the Crusaders, with a few broken Corinthian columns. There is nothing now but the name "Saelin," and the wretched Arab village, to indicate the site of the ancient Jewish city. In fact, it seems to have been entirely lost sight of in history from the time of its destruction by the Philistines, and its being held up as a warning to the people in the seventh chapter of Jeremiah, until some late writers settled the question of its situation, of which there can now be little doubt, partly from its present name, and from its situation as described in Judges xxi. 19—the "place which is on the north side of Beth-el, and on the highway that goeth up from Beth-el to Shechem." On this hill, on which the ruins and a few mud huts of the Arabs are situated, and down its gentle slopes, one may well imagine what this land was in the days of Israel's strength, and the contrast of what it is now. Then these broken terraces were richly cultivated and clothed with fig, vine, and olive. Now the hill-side represents nothing but barren rock and stunted vegetation. Towards noon the day cleared up, and we were able to enjoy the scenery, which is as fine as any in Palestine.

CHAPTER XIII

WE now come "on that highway that goeth up from Bethel to Shechem, and on the south of Lebonah." The hill-sides were clothed with olives and cultivated terraces, presenting a more healthy appearance than anything we had seen on this journey; and as we approached Nabulus, riding along the slopes of Mount Gerizim, the scenery became magnificent. Below us was a long fertile valley, which needed nothing but good farmsteading to give it the appearance of some of our own rich straths; but here there is no safe home for the farmer, who has to carry his plough and produce to those miserable villages perched on the face of the hill, where he can find safety both for his small flock and for his crop. Before entering the Valley of Nabulus, we made a short detour to " Jacob's Well," memorable for the interview between our Saviour and the woman of Samaria. This is now surrounded with ruins. Under a broken arch is a vault or cave, such as we see everywhere through Palestine. At the

bottom of the vault is the mouth of the well. We
were told that this was some fifty or sixty feet deep.
We threw down some stones, and found there was
water at the bottom, but no use is now made of it.

We next proceeded up the richly watered and
cultivated valley to the city, and not venturing to
pitch our tents, we took up our quarters at a large
and comfortable khan. This being Sunday, we enjoyed the rest of the day, and read up our Bible
history and scriptural events. Next morning, our
dragoman informed us that the tents, etc., were so
saturated and heavy, that it was necessary to have
them dried, and as the day proved fine, we took
advantage of the sunshine to turn out our books and
linen for the same purpose. At noon, we ascended
Mount Gerizim to see the ruins of the Temple, and
the place where the Samaritans still hold the Pass-
over. This is a hard pull on foot, being more than
1,000 feet above the town, and over a steep and
rugged road. We might have had donkeys, but did
not estimate the difficulties of the journey. The
present massive ruins have nothing of the Jewish
character about them, but are Roman, and the foundations of a Christian church may be as late as the
period of the Crusaders. The summit is covered
with extensive ruins. The large stones pointed out

as covering those that were brought up by Joshua
from the Jordan, have more the appearance of
scarped rock than natural stones. The view from
the summit of the mountain is among the finest and
most extensive in Palestine.

I was fortunate enough to have an introduction to
M. Fallscheer, who is in charge of Bishop Gobat's
school. After we had heard the boys read portions of the Scriptures in Arabic and English, and
sing an English hymn, he was good enough to be
our guide through the city. There are few objects
of sufficient interest to reward one for wading
through the narrow and dirty streets. There is
throughout the town and valley a profusion of
water, but instead of being guided by aqueducts for
use and ornament, much of it is allowed to run at
large, mingling with accumulated dirt and offal, till
the streets become almost impassable. They have a
number of marble fountains or troughs throughout
the city, which from their style of ornamentation
seem to have been Greek and Roman sarcophagi.
This profusion of fine water renders the whole
valley rich and fertile. The olive, orange, lemon,
and fig trees yield abundant crops, and all table
vegetables are cheap and plentiful; and in the hands
of an industrious people, and a just and liberal

government, the beauty of this valley would be unrivalled. Groping our way through dark arches,
and along the margin of open sewers, we reached
the Samaritan synagogue. The old rabbi, a man of
pleasing manners and intelligence, received us very
kindly, led us into the synagogue, and brought out
the celebrated scroll from behind the screen, or altar.
This scroll is said to be very ancient, and is a copy
of the "Pentateuch." The depth of the parchment
is about fourteen inches, and it is said to measure
about eighty feet. It is rolled on two metal bars,
and enclosed in a silver embossed case, which bears
the appearance of Venetian art of the 12th or 13th
century. He offered to show us several other ancient
MSS., but our curiosity was satisfied with the one
to which I have referred. It is a poor, small, and
bare building, and forms the residence of the rabbi
and his family. There are altogether about 150
Samaritans in Nabulus, and one wonders how these
few, so intelligent and enterprising, should have
held so long to their ancient traditions, as they were
not Jews or bound to the Jewish faith. The Crusaders
have here, as elsewhere, left some relics of their
perverted Christianity. Their church is now an
empty neglected mosque ; near it there is a building
called "the Crusader's Tower," of the same date,

from the top of which we had a fine view of the
city, and down the green valley as far as "Jacob's
Well," and the slopes of the two mountains, Gerizim
and Ebal. This is one of the most ancient cities
mentioned in sacred history. Here Abraham
first pitched his tent, in "the Land of Canaan."
The modern town of Neopolis, corrupted into
Nablous, or Nabulus, founded by the Romans in the
time of Vespasian, is well up the valley between the
two mountains; but it is generally believed that the
ancient Shechem lay farther down, towards the
mouth of the valley, where "Jacob's Well," to
which the woman came to draw water, and the
"Tomb of Joseph," would be in the immediate
vicinity of the town.

M. Fallscheer informed me that the population is
increasing since the cotton trade sprang up, and is
now estimated at 14,000, of whom about 1,000 are
Christians. I found none of that fanaticism among
the Mohammedan inhabitants to which former travellers have referred. We walked through the
bazaars, peeped into the courts of their houses and
mosques, and chatted with the inhabitants, through
our interpreter, without any symptoms of insolence
or insult.

Our dragoman and his men were glad of these

two days' rest, as it enabled them to get their tents
and coverings dried, and to lay in some provisions.

On Tuesday morning, the 15th December, we
started at 7.30 A.M., horses, mules, and donkeys all
in good working order, and Mustaffa, the cook, and
refractory muleteer, in better humour than they
had been for some days. A ride of two hours
brought us to Samaria. The day was fine, and we
were able to spend an hour pleasantly among the
ruins of this ancient capital. The "Hill of Samaria" occupies a very fine and commanding situation, rising about 600 feet above the surrounding
valleys, in a semicircle, and a succession of neglected
terraces. I need scarcely refer to the Bible history
of the city which crowned this hill. Those familiar
with the sacred volume will remember that it was
long the capital of the ten tribes, and must have
been both a strong and populous city, as it resisted
the powerful army of the Assyrians for three years.
From the time of its destruction, we hear nothing
but of its guilt and condemnation, till its history is
revived by Josephus in his glowing description of
this magnificent city of Herod, which he called
Sebaste. The most prominent and interesting ruins
now to be seen are those of St. John's Church of
the Crusaders. This building still retains its gene-

ral outline, and is one of the best specimens of the
architecture of that period now in Palestine.   There
was no unwillingness on the part of our Moslem
guide to show us over the entire building, though
it is now a mosque.   We were only asked to sub-
stitute slippers for our shoes, when we descended to
the Grotto, or Sepulchre of St. John the Baptist.
This cave is similar to many that we have already
seen and attempted to describe, with six or eight
loculi for the dead.   One is staggered at every turn
in the journey of Palestine by the many conflicting
traditions.   Certain Christians and Mohammedans
tell you that this is the burial-place of St. John,
while the priests of the Armenian Church of Jerusalem show the pilgrims the place of his inter-
ment, over which they have an altar.   Perhaps this
uncertainty is not without its uses, when we see
how prone man is to fall into material worship.
The ruins cover the plateau of a richly-cultivated
hill, round which for a distance of two miles
there is a succession of stone and marble columns,
prostrate and upright, or partly sunk in the earth;
most of them without their capitals, which may be
seen in broken fragments strewed along the ground.
The present miserable Arab village, consisting of
forty or fifty huts, lies on the face of the hill near

the Church of St. John, and is characteristic of the dirt and indolence of this misgoverned country.

From Nabulus northward, the cultivation and scenery became more changed and interesting. About an hour's ride beyond Samaria we ascended a ridge, from which we had a varied and extensive view over mountain and valley, each hill being crowned with a picturesque village, and cultivated terraces. Here we spread our carpet for lunch, and then had a very enjoyable ride on to Jenîn, the En-gannim of the Bible. Our muleteer had not pitched our tent, but had procured for us a small upper room in the outskirts of the village. The comforts and discomforts of life are in a great degree comparative. This little apartment of 9 feet square, with a small wooden shutter for a window, and cold stone floor, would have appeared very wretched to a man that had just left his club or comfortable English home, but to us, after our experience on this journey, it was almost a luxury. We got our three small beds ranged round the sides, and then there was just room for our little table in the centre. The cook and Mustaffa found a place below, and were able to get up a very good dinner. The neighbourhood was too dirty and unsafe for us to venture out in the evening.

Next morning the weather was favourable, and soon after daylight we mounted our horses. We were delighted with the beautiful and picturesque scenery before us. This day was rich in Biblical history. There lay the broad and rich Plain of Esdraelon. It was a relief to get out of the dirty Arab village, and to gaze on the beauties that nature had spread around. The hills are here better clothed, and the plains broad and fertile; but the ancient terraces are worn and washed away, and the rich plains are left uncultivated, save in little patches here and there.

If the reader will refer to a map he will find that this Plain of Esdraelon—or Valley of Jezreel, or Plain of Megiddo, for these are one and the same 'place—stretches from the Jordan on the east, and narrowing towards Mount Carmel, descends to the Mediterranean. It is one of the largest as well as the most fertile tracts in Palestine.

When riding over the comparative barren hills around Jerusalem one has difficulty in reconciling the constant allusions, in the poetical and historical passages of the Old Testament, to the beauty and richness of "The Promised Land," with the sight now presented to view. This "overflowing" richness is only understood when we come to traverse those great plains and intersecting valleys that divide the mountain ranges. The rains had now set in, and the whole of this vast plain was one sheet of rich colour, from the beautiful scarlet anemone to the white jonquil, and crocus, amidst a mass of rank vegetation ; security and cultivation only are needed to render this the most fertile spot on earth ; but here they have neither. The poor fellah may labour and sow, but the fruits of his toil will be wrung out of him by the greedy and dishonest sheik, or plundered by the lawless Bedouin. We made a short detour to the right, to the Fountain of Jezreel, which flows in a copious stream of fine clear water from the base of Mount Gilboa, near to where the Israelites' pitched their tents, and from the ridge of which Gideon descended and overthrew the Midianites with "the sword of the Lord."

We did not go on to the village of Jezreel, as we learned that it would not reward the labour, but proceeded north through the valley, leaving, at a little distance on our left the village of El-Fûleh, a stronghold of the Crusaders, and the battle-ground of the French and Turks in 1799, in what was called "the battle of Mount Tabor."

We now passed round the base of "Little Her-

mon," and ascended the ridge on which the village
of Nain stands, ever memorable for the example of
our Saviour's love. (Luke vii.) We sat down outside the village on a small plateau of limestone, and
had our lunch, and then a stroll round the village.
There is nothing now to mark the site of the old
city except a few Arab huts; but the empty tombs,
caves, and cisterns, which cover a considerable space
round the present village, indicate that there must
have been a town of some size and importance at one
time on this ridge.

From our resting-place we had another fine view
of some of those spots the names of which are so
familiar to us. We had behind us Little Hermon,
and immediately before us Mount Tabor, and far in
the distance the snowy peak of Mount Hermon. I
confess I was a little disappointed with Mount
Tabor. Seen from the south where we stood, it
forms an exact portion of a circle, but does not
appear to be more than 600 feet above the plain,
though I believe it is more than 1,000 feet in height.
We did not ascend the mountain, but pushed on
over the plains to Nazareth.

CHAPTER XIV.

As we approached the ridge of lofty hills that hide
Nazareth from view, we began to think that Mustaffa
had lost his way, but he pointed to an almost per-
pendicular hill and told us that was the road to
the city. There seemed no passage between the
projecting cliffs and great boulders which hung on
the face of the mountain, but while we were gazing
on the scene in some doubt, we saw a woman and
a donkey emerging from between two of these
boulders; so concluding there must be a passage
somewhere, we commenced our ascent. Mustaffa
and my two companions soon dismounted, and led
their horses. I had by this time gained such confidence in my little horse, that I would almost have
trusted him to take me up the face of a wall, but as
I neared the top I dismounted to take a view over
the plains we had left, and then for the first time
saw the extent of our danger, and that I had perhaps
been a little foolhardy. One false step would have
precipitated man and horse nearly a thousand feet

without a chance of escape. The view from the summit of this hill was magnificent, embracing Mount Tabor, and all the range of the "hills of Galilee," down to Mount Carmel and the Mediterranean; and on the opposite slopes and valley we came in sight of the sacred city, rising in broken clusters of buildings from the rich green valley below. We descended, and for the first time on this journey pitched our tents, on a small green plot near the "Fountain of the Virgin."

We had still some hours of daylight, and while our men were unpacking, and getting the dinner ready, we started to hear the service in the church of the Latin Convent. Here Rome has it all to herself, and there is an order, grandeur, and dignity about this shrine, that throws the Church of the Holy Sepulchre into the shade. Here the eye and senses are pleased; in the other, every sense of religion, taste, and propriety is violated. The music was superb, and conducted with solemn grandeur. The great altar is at the bottom of a broad flight of steps richly ornamented, and illuminated with gilt and silver lamps. The priests in their rich sacerdotal trappings, the floating incense, and chanting of the choir, and the solemnity of the place, subdued the heart, and

N

brought moisture to the eyes.   Whatever may be
the errors and perversions of Rome, this was not
the moment to question them.   We knew that we
were within the narrow circle where our Divine
Redeemer spent His youth in the humble home of
His earthly parents, and that He was familiar with
all the scenes around this valley.   This church is
alleged to be on the site of the house of Mary the
mother of our Lord.   Those who take any interest in
the extravagances of the Roman Church will remember that the original house "was conveyed by
angels to Loretto," and that over it a magnificent
church has been built, to which thousands of pilgrims
now resort.

There is no place in Palestine, with the exception
of Jerusalem, which inspires one with such deep
interest as Nazareth.   Not in itself, for it seems to
have been a small and unimportant village, not
once mentioned in the Old Testament; but because
it is entirely bound up in our common Christianity,
and with which its name is identified.

There is little of interest in modern Nazareth, if
we dismiss those traditional places about which the
Greek and Latin Churches contend; such as the
Annunciation, the Grotto, the workshop of Joseph,
the dining-table of our Lord, and some others,

pointed out by guides and monks. In the case of the Annunciation, these churches have each a separate shrine. I have already referred to that of the Latins. The Greeks have their Church of the Annunciation outside the town, near the Fountain of the Virgin, where they say the salutation of the angel came to Mary when she was drawing water from this fountain.

We were soon tired of these sights, and glad to remount our horses, and get out of the dirty, narrow, and unpaved streets, and breathe the fresh air of the mountain.

We ascended the heights, on the base of which the village rests, and were rewarded with one of the finest views in Palestine, embracing the whole ·range of hill and vale from the Mediterranean to the Jordan. We were now on the highest point of "the Hills of Galilee." A number of these converge towards the fertile valley of Nazareth, and have more verdure and beauty than the more rugged mountains of Judah and Ephraim.

On returning to our tents we passed more than one precipice overlooking the village, which may have been that to which the populace led our Saviour, "that they might cast him down headlong."

It was impossible in so short a time to form any correct idea of the character, number, and occupation of the inhabitants.   They are chiefly Christians, and may altogether be estimated at 3,500 to 4,000, of whom there may be of Greek and Roman Christians 3,000, Maronites 500, and about the same number of Moslems.   The men and women look more healthy and active, and in every respect superior in dress and appearance to those of purely Moslem cities.

I had letters to the Protestant mission, and was sorry that I had not an opportunity of seeing the school, as the superintendent was unwell; but I had a very kind reception from Dr. Vartan, the medical missionary from Scotland, and his excellent Scotch wife.   This gentleman has not yet matured his plans, but from what I saw and heard of his missionary character and professional kindness, I am quite sure that his services will be of great value. When we returned to our tent the night again looked stormy, and as I was still suffering from effects of fatigue, Dr. Vartan suggested that I should go to the Latin Convent for the night, which I did, and I found a clean and comfortable room. Here I met the Rev. Mr. Follet, of Christ Church, Oxford, and Dr. Torry, of New York, and his two nieces; they had been travelling and suffering like ourselves, and doubted if they were well enough to proceed. Next morning, after a comfortable breakfast at the Convent, I joined my friends, who were packing and striking the tents, and at 8.30 A.M. we joined Dr. Torry's party, who had determined to cross over to Tiberias. The day was stormy, and two of our number were suffering a good deal from late exposure. The distance from Nazareth to Tiberias is about fifteen miles, every foot of which· seems sacred ground. On our right was Mount Tabor, and on our left Cana of Galilee. Along this road, to His second home of Capernaum, our Lord and His disciples must often have travelled. Unfortunately for us, the weather was by no means favourable for serious contemplation.

We took shelter and lunched in a little khan at Lûbieh, and soon after passed Hattîn, the last battle-field of the Crusaders. The reader of history will remember how the dishonesty of the Christian warriors roused the indignation of the chivalrous Saladin, and that he attacked their army near this place, and almost annihilated the "defenders of the Holy Cross." At 3 P.M. we arrived at Tiberias. Our dragomans had provided separate quarters for both parties, uncomfortable enough, but we were glad to get any shelter.

To describe this town would be little but a repetition of what I have already said on other occasions, except that it is at the lowest depth that any human habitation can reach. There is no attempt at draining or paving the narrow streets. We attempted to walk out to see the place, but the heavy rains had stirred up all manner of abominations, and we could not proceed a step without being nearly up to the knees in wet and filth. We had therefore to make the best of our small quarters, an upper room of 10 feet square, with open shutters, but no windows. Mustaffa was provided with charcoal, and we got a little fire in the middle of the room to dispel the damp till the cook got our dinner ready, when he surprised us as usual with his wonderful resources. And now, being "by the Sea of Galilee," we spent the evening in reading and talking over the events that had transpired around this spot. There are few places richer in associations, and as we recalled these events to memory, the imagination vividly pictured the fishermen leaving their nets to follow Christ, and the crowds listening to His discourses on the shore.

It is very disappointing to find that there are no "fishermen" and no "ships" on the sea of Galilee. On inquiry we found that there was only one small boat on the lake. We sent for the proprietor to know his time and terms, but the cunning old fox had already been in treaty *with the other party, and demanded forty francs for two or three hours' use of his boat. We learned from our dragoman that he was making the same heavy demand on our friends; in fact, with all the tact of his race, was trying to play the one party against the other: as there were ladies in the case, we gave up our object and let them make their own terms. At sunrise next morning we had our horses brought up and rode down the side of the lake, through the ruins of the ancient city to the hot baths mentioned by Josephus. There are four or five of these hot sulphur springs that flow from the base of the hills that skirt the lake. Over two of them are square buildings and domes in a ruinous condition, and the water is collected in cisterns. We entered one of these and stripped, but found we could not endure the heat, which was about 150° Fahr. We could only lie on the margin of the pool, and use the water cautiously. I imagine that I found great relief from this process, and before I dressed I ran down the banks and had a comfortable bathe in the lake.

From the ruins that are scattered about, and the

fragments of thick walls that run down into the
lake, it is evident that the Herodian-Roman city
lay to the south of the modern one. The whole of
this tract, from the mountains north of the sea of
Galilee to the Dead Sea, has suffered severely from
earthquakes, a fact which helps to account for the
total destruction of so many ancient cities mentioned
in Scripture. As late as 1837 one of these sad
catastrophes occurred, in which several cities round
the lake were destroyed, and many thousands of
the inhabitants perished. The old castle and the
walls were shattered and thrown down, and as the
Turks never repair anything, they still lie in the
same state. The town altogether presents a sad
scene of desolation, and has sunk down into a
miserable village of 2,000 inhabitants, of whom
nearly half are Jews, of a more squalid appearance,
if possible, than those I have described in Jerusalem.

It was a great disappointment to me that we could
not spend a day on the Lake of Gennesaret and
visit the supposed sites of Magdala, Capernaum,
Chorazin, and Bethsaida, but my American friends
were tied to time, and wished to push on to catch
the steamer passing Haifa. Perhaps the reader will
not lose much by my disappointment, as there is no

THE SEA OF GALILEE

certainty whatever regarding the position of these cities. It is sufficient to know that along the northern side of the lake there stood several cities of some importance, inhabited by a hardy and intelligent race, engaged as agriculturists and fishermen.

We know that from the latter our Saviour chose His disciples, and there is sufficient proof that these men were superior in education and other advantages to many of the same class and position in the present day. They may have gained some knowledge of Greek and Latin from their conquerors, and were familiar with their own Scriptures, and, humanly speaking, were just the men suited to the great and important work to which their Master had called them.

If any of my readers should desire any further information on these interesting localities, the Sea of Tiberias, or the source and course of the Jordan, they cannot do better than consult the volume of "Rob Roy on the Jordan." The courageous and persevering author of this book, whom Mr. Spurgeon justly describes as "a man who can serve his God and paddle his own canoe," has given a vivid and graphic description of his voyage and its results. They will learn that to the south of Mount Hermon a spring issues, forming a rivulet, called at its source the Hasbany. This river unites with another called Bánias, and both are lost in a morass, and permeating for a time through swamps and jungles, reach the Lake Holeh, or "Waters of Merom," out of which the Jordan again flows southward for twenty miles, when it enters the Sea of Galilee at its north-east point, and passing through the lake descends, through winding, muddy banks, for sixty miles, when it is lost in the Dead Sea.

The four cities referred to in Scripture lay along the north-west shores of the lake. Some writers have placed them in this order: Magdala, a few miles to the north of Tiberias; beyond this Bethsaida; then Capernaum; and at the north point Chorazin. Captains Wilson and Anderson have discovered some interesting ruins at these places; but as the learned writers on this subject cannot agree on the real sites of these cities or villages, it would scarcely be profitable to discuss the matter here.

We despatched our mules and baggage in the morning, and started a little before noon to cross to Acre. Leaving "Cana of Galilee" on our right, we arrived at Kefr Menda at sunset, before reaching which we were nearly lost in a swamp; two of our

horses sank nearly out of sight, and it was with
great difficulty we got them out. It was dusk
before we reached our evening quarters. We procured accommodation at a small khan or shed outside the village. We found our muleteers had
arrived some time before us, by a much easier and
safer passage, and we began to fear that the route
was new to our dragoman, and thought we were
fortunate in getting so easily over it. Our next
day's journey was to Acre, or Akka. The greater
part of the road was over and along the face of the
mountains, so that we had no difficulties to contend
with. When we came to the high mountains that
overlook the plains of Akka, and the beautiful and
then calm Mediterranean, and saw the smoke of
the distant steamers, it was the most joyful and
refreshing sight we had seen since we left
Jerusalem, and we longed to be again on the
blue waters.

We found the whole plains of Akka a sheet of
water and marsh, and had to make a detour of two
hours to get down upon the coast. The river Belus,
now called N'amân, which runs through into the
bay under the walls of the city, was very high, and
after some delay we procured a boat to carry ourselves and luggage across. The mules were un-

loaded, and with some difficulty were led through the stream. We had a consultation whether we should pitch our tents on the sands or enter the town. My friends were inclined for the former, and I had no desire to enter this den of abomination, which I had seen in passing a short time before; but the evening looked very stormy, and I knew if it came on to blow there would be little safety for us and our tents on the sands. Very fortunately for us, as it turned out, we abandoned the idea of encamping outside, and entered the city, where we got comfortable quarters in the public khan, as well for ourselves as for our cook, dragoman, etc. We had not been long settled down in our comparatively comfortable quarters when our worst expectations were realised. The wind rose to a gale, accompanied by a torrent of rain that must have swept our tents and baggage into the sea, and we had reason to congratulate ourselves that we were under the shelter of stone walls.

There is nothing in this garrison city that would lead any one to remain in it longer than necessary. In the morning we strolled through its dirty bazaars and unpaved streets, and ascended the ramparts of the old castle that overlooks the sea. These are almost in the same state as they were left after the bombardment of 1840. The guns are corroded with rust, and seem not to have been touched for years, and the heaps of shot that lie beside them are now a mere mass of oxidized iron. The town, garrison, walls, and ramparts are perfect types of Moslem neglect and decay. There are some relics·still remaining to remind one of the city of the Knights of St. John, from which it derives its Christian name, viz., the ruins of St. Andrew's Church, the Hotel of the Knights Hospitallers, and the Church of St. John, now the Latin Convent. These, and the ruins of the old fortifications, are all that tell of the St. Jean D'Acre of the Crusaders. The city has now sunk down to 4,500 inhabitants; but its old associations, as the landing-place and last refuge of the Crusaders, will always invest it with interest.

This was our settling-day with our escort—a time generally attended with a good deal of haggling and discontent; but on this score we had nothing to complain of. Mustaffa behaved like a gentleman. Our engagement was for ten days, more or less, according to the direction of our journey, which was entirely at our own disposal. This was now the ninth day that we were out, and as we were going to Haifa to wait for a steamer, we did not require an escort any longer. The whole charge for the journey was £32.* We had paid half this sum on leaving Jerusalem, and the balance was now cheerfully paid and frankly received without any importunity. The old cook, who had suffered most and served us the best, had a douceur. We were able to give them all a good character, as they had served us honestly and faithfully under rather trying circumstances. It was arranged that our dragoman should accompany us to Haifa, to take back our horses and baggage mules to Akka, and return with his companions to Jerusalem.

The morning turned out fine, and we started at noon. The circle of the bay from the point of Akka to Haifa at the base of Mount Carmel is about twelve miles. We had again some difficulty in crossing the Belus, which, taking its rise in the marshes of the plain, swells rapidly after heavy rains. We procured a boat for ourselves, but had hard work to induce our horses and mules to take the water, which was now nearly up to their ears. Our road lay for several miles across the sands. The two ships which I saw driven on shore some six weeks before, with other *débris*, were strewed along the coast. We were amused with the dex-

---

* Or about £1 a·day each.

terity of the fishermen in the use of their hand nets.
These are bell shaped; a rope is fixed to the top,
and round the border of the nets are attached leaden
weights, and as the sea rolls back they watch their
opportunity and throw the net in to a considerable
distance; the weights sink the net, which secures
all within its range. They had been labouring all
the morning and caught nothing. Here we had
a little episode which might have given us trouble.
One of our party got off his horse to look at something, when the horse slipped the rein out of his
hand and started over the sands to the open plain.
Mustaffa and I had been lingering behind, watching
the fishermen, and when we pushed on we found
the deacon in pursuit of his horse, and the priest
jogging on, either ignorant of or indifferent to his
friend's dilemma. I had seen a similar thing before
in the Valley of the Jordan, where the horse of one
of our party made its escape, and every attempt to
catch him seemed futile, till our young Bedouin
guide, who was splendidly mounted, went after him
like a hound after a hare, and literally rode him
down. Mustaffa seemed equally alive to the difficulty, and we immediately started in pursuit of the
animal. I directed Mustaffa to make a circle round
the off-side, that we might meet in front of him and

turn his course. This we tried four or five times. At length we turned his head inward, and getting near, I made a dash and caught the 'bridle with the end of my umbrella. We now arrived at the ancient Kishon. When I passed this coast six weeks before, the people were crossing the sands, and there was no appearance of a river. This curious phenomenon requires a little explanation. The sands roll in here in a great body, and in the dry season close the mouth of the river, which then spreads into marshes, and finds its way to the sea through the sand. The river was now swollen beyond its usual bounds, and it was a question for some time whether we could get our cattle across. By proceeding higher up we found a boat, in which we got ourselves and luggage over; but it was an hour before we could get our horses to take the water.

On reaching Haifa, we took up our quarters at the Russian hospice, where everything was clean and comfortable; and after some refreshment, we procured donkeys, and started off for the Convent on Mount Carmel, about half an hour's distance from the shore. This Convent is a conspicuous object from sea and land, standing as it does on the extreme ridge of the mountain. The modern build-

MOUNT CARMEL.

ing was raised by the efforts of one man—one of the brothers, who preached a sort of crusade through Europe to raise funds for rebuilding the Convent, and collected £20,000 sterling. The present structure has no equal in Palestine, except perhaps that of the Russian hospice, church, and hospital at Jerusalem. It forms a large square building, with the church in the centre, where we are shown the Cave of Elijah and the Grotto of Elisha. In company of one of the brothers, I walked out on the spur of the mountain to view the magnificent scenery around, I was able to look back on the Valley of Esdraelon, where we had encountered so many difficulties; down over the plains of Sharon and the coast towns of Tyre and Sidon, and away to the north-east, to the lofty peak of Hermon and the snowy ridge of the distant Lebanon, while under our eye was the wide expanse of the Mediterranean.

The Austrian Lloyds' steamer was expected to pass about 6 P.M. We hurried back to Haifa while it was daylight. The boat only remains two hours in the harbour; so that we were kept up all night in anxiety, as she did not make her appearance till seven o'clock the following morning, when we embarked for Beyrout. The distance is seven hours, and the charge twenty-five francs. My

o

friends were under the impression that this high charge included the dinner we had on board, but were charged four francs extra, to which they made strong objections. Passing Tyre and Sidon near enough to scrutinise them with our glasses, we arrived at Beyrout at 4 p.m., and proceeded to my former comfortable quarters, the "Oriental Hotel." My further acquaintance with the Maronite proprietor but confirmed my first favourable impressions. My two American companions were so distressed and disgusted with the journey, that nothing could have induced them to prolong their stay in Palestine, and they took a passage by the French steamer, which passed next morning, for Alexandria. It has been my good fortune to travel with American gentlemen through all parts of the world, and I have always found them agreeable, intelligent, and communicative, ready to laugh at troubles or to overcome them, and neglecting no opportunity for rational enjoyment and information. I found my two companions no exception to this rule, and parted from them with great regret. I was still suffering from low fever and otherwise unwell, and they urged me to accompany them; but I had determined, at all risks, to carry out my programme, and engaged a place in the diligence for Damascus.

CHAPTER XV.

A FRENCH company have formed a very good road across the Lebanon, and run a diligence daily to and from Damascus. The fare for the coupé is thirty francs, and for the interior, or banquette, twenty-two francs. The distance is about eighty-four miles, and is accomplished in fourteen hours. The diligence starts punctually at 4 A.M., and at half-past two, when I got up, the rain was falling in torrents. The starting-place was some distance out of town, and as you cannot call a cab in Syria, there was nothing left for me but to trudge through the dirty flooded streets to the station, preceded by a servant carrying a lantern. I found I had got the coupé all to myself; the interior was filled with Greek and Arab merchants. As we ascended the mountains the day cleared up. The snow lay along the roadside, the air was dry and bracing, and I soon felt something like new life and vigour. Oddly enough, I was crossing the Pyrenees in a similar manner on the same day the year before, in a like unwieldy conveyance, with a team of eight horses and mules; but here the Frenchmen have been able to drill a little more life into the Arab than into the indolent self-sufficient Spaniard. There are no great feats of engineering here, but the road is admirable, and constructed with great skill, economy, and safety. Here is a proof, if proof were wanted, of the difference between honest scientific labour and the ignorance and dishonesty of semi-barbarism. I have referred in a former chapter to the road the Turks are now constructing from Jaffa to Jerusalem. For this work the heads of families, from Hebron to Nabulus, have been taxed; already upwards of £60,000 have been raised, and this tax may go on to any amount. In the meantime this short road of thirty-two miles is "dragging its slow length along" by a species of forced labour, and is so badly done that the whole will have to be reconstructed. This much in honour of the French and in acknowledgment of their services. We ascended to the height of nearly 6,000 feet. The scenery in many parts was grand and picturesque. The slopes of the mountains were better cultivated, and the villages very superior to those in the south. As we approached Damascus, the scenery through the Valley of the Abana and the broad rich plains lying before us was magnificent.

We reached Damascus in comfort at 6 P.M., and found the waiter from Dimitre's Hotel in attendance, who conducted us to that large and comfortable house. The proprietor is a fine type of the pushing enterprising Greek, and, like most of his compatriots in the East, has had his reward. They were all in a very sad way at this time. The order had just been received from the Turkish Government for the expulsion of all Greeks. Many of them held considerable property, and they were condemning their own Government and the men of Athens in no measured terms of abuse. "There will be no rest and safety for us," said an influential Greek to me, "till we hang half-a-dozen of these pedantic and restless scholars of Athens."

Next morning I waited on Mr. Rogers, the British consul, to whom I had an introduction. This gentleman is so well known in the East, that anything I might add respecting him would be superfluous, and might be considered obtrusive; suffice it to say, that he offered me his dragoman, and gave me all necessary instructions to see the city to the best advantage during the two days I proposed remaining there. I had three personal disappointments. I had hoped to overtake Mr. Gaze's party, who had made a successful and comfortable tour through Palestine, and to have accompanied them to Baalbek, but found they had passed on some days before. I also hoped to meet Mrs. Thompson,* whose schools I had visited at Beyrout, but found that lady had left on the morning of my arrival for her schools in the Lebanon ; and, though last, not least, I also hoped to pay my respects to the commander of the "Rob Roy," whom we all respect and esteem so highly: he also left on the morning of my arrival, on his journey to the source of the Jordan.

Armed with the consul's authority, we commenced our explorations at the old castle to the west of the town. It covers a considerable space, and is well protected by walls and moat. The architecture is of a mixed character, some of which may be anterior to the Roman period. We then proceeded to the great mosque, and were admitted with an order on the payment of ten francs each. A great change has taken place here, as well as at other cities throughout the Mussulman dominions, and there is now much less jealousy or fanaticism. I considered it a great privilege to be allowed to go over this

---

* Since this journal was closed, this excellent and benevolent lady has gone to her reward, after a life of most exemplary labour and Christian love.

building, as there is a greater variety of study for the archæologist here than even on the platform of the Haram at Jerusalem. There is every specimen here of architecture, from the earliest Jewish, or Cyclopean, down through the Greek and Roman to the beautiful Arabesque of the Saracens. The building still retains many of the marks of the Christian cathedral, with its long aisles and ranges of Corinthian columns, and tesselated marble flooring.

"The street called Straight," which we next visited, has entirely lost its original character. It has been encroached upon by stalls and shades, and is nothing better than a very dirty alley. Proceeding along this narrow street, which intersects the city from east to west, we passed through the Christian quarter, and saw the signs of the destruction wrought during the fanatical outbreak of 1860. The heartrending scenes of that time are now almost forgotten, except among the surviving sufferers; but the event has shaken all confidence in what is called Mohammedan liberality and progress. The Christians say, very justly, that they have no security against such fearful outrages; and that the boasted liberty of the Turks is merely a passive indifference. Nor must we confound this movement with the disturbances between the Druses

and Maronites in the Lebanon. These were warlike
people accustomed to arms, and to defend themselves, while the Christians of Damascus were un-
armed, and totally innocent of all aggression. No
one can visit this spot without feelings of sorrow
and indignation; sorrow for the poor defenceless
victims, and indignation at the savage outrage per-
petrated under the eye of the garrison, and with
the sanction of the officers of a government for which,
only four short years before, we had poured out our
blood and treasure to save it from annihilation !

Passing onward, we go through the eastern gate
of the city. This is the ancient Roman gate, consisting of one large and two lesser arches. The
latter are built up, and there is little else remaining
of the original walls. Those now surrounding the
city are Saracenic, and are weak and neglected. A
little beyond this gate is a mound walled over, containing the remains of some 2,500 of the victims of
the three days' massacre ; and a little farther to
the right is the English burying-ground, a small
walled enclosure, in which I noticed a memorial
stone over the grave of the well-known author of
the "History of Civilisation in Europe" (erected, if
I mistake not, by and at the expense of Mr. Rogers,
late consul at Damascus). I was quite unprepared

for this discovery, but learned that Mr. Buckle was attacked while here with the "Syrian fever," and cut off in the midst of his labours.

It is not over the grave of this great scholar and philosopher, that I dare trust myself to offer an opinion of his services to history and literature. There are few who have had the courage to speak out so boldly as this writer. Perhaps there are great truths which history and experience teach us, but which we are afraid to whisper even to ourselves; hence this able and laborious author may have laid his memory open to unfavourable criticism, such as all honest historians must do who have the courage to speak out boldly on the crimes and errors of the past.

Returning towards the city, a built-up door in the wall, on a level with the ground, was pointed out by our guide as the window from which "St. Paul was lowered over a wall in a basket." This is neither the wall nor the window, but let that pass; it serves to recall the event to our memory, though that is scarcely necessary, as no one can visit this city without vividly realising this memorable incident. I have endeavoured to confine myself as much as possible in these letters to the simple details of my own journey and experience, but it is difficult to leave Damascus without some reference to St. Paul; and I hope the reader will not consider it presumptuous in a layman, to devote a few lines in pious reverence to the memory of the great Apostle of the Gentiles. Indeed, we could not avoid the subject if we would, for we are reminded of his travels, and teaching, and sufferings, in every step of this journey—from Athens, Asia Minor, among the islands, along the coast of Syria, and to and from Jerusalem. Of all the apostles, he is the one most constantly before our mind's eye, and whose life and labours we seem best to understand and appreciate. There may be a little hero-worship here, for he gave up, in a worldly sense, more than all the other apostles. His learning astonished Festus, a Roman scholar, and his eloquence "almost persuaded King Agrippa to be a Christian." The learned and critical Athenians were moved by his earnest and impassioned address, and "promised to hear him again on this matter." His learning and influence among his own countrymen, or even with the Judæo-Roman government, might have led to power and distinction. All this he sacrificed, and "counted as dross, that he might win Christ." How refreshing it is, after witnessing the idolatry and perverted Christianity of the East, to turn to his epistles and the Acts of the Apostles, and know there what Christianity is! St. Paul had everything to gain in social position, influence, and worldly honour, by opposing the new faith ; all of which he abandoned, and from the day of his miraculous conversion, within sight of this city, he entered on his sacred work, and for thirty years toiled in poverty, through sufferings and endless persecution, with a heroism that must win the admiration of the most indifferent sceptic. But it is not only his heroism and self-sacrifices that win upon us, but his unbounded love and affection, which formed so great an attribute in the life of his Divine Master. There is charity and love in every sentence that comes from his lips. Even in his reproofs there were "charity and love." Though he "laboured that he might not be a burthen on the brethren, and ministered to them that were with him," still it is in love and charity—that "charity which suffereth long, and is kind," which "envieth not, vaunteth not itself, and is not puffed up." So strongly are these simple and sublime lessons impressed on the Christian mind, that one might almost say, if there were no other evidence of the truth of our Saviour's mission on earth than that given by St. Paul, it would be sufficient to prove the Divine revelation of God to man.

The city now is a sad caricature of the Damascus
of the eastern poets, and is among the dirtiest of all
the Turco-Arabic towns. The streets are narrow,
unpaved, and impassable except on horseback. I
tried to make my way on foot through the mud and
filth, but was at last obliged to get on the back of a
donkey. The celebrated bazaars are a disappointment; the stalls or ducans are chiefly supplied with
inferior European goods, and are neither better nor
worse than those of Cairo and old Stamboul. Perhaps I ought to make an exception of the silver-
smiths and jewellers' bazaar. This covers a large
area, and has raised platforms where each artisan
has his small bellows and charcoal fire; the great
variety of tasteful filigree work exhibited is pretty,
and very tempting to those who have money to
spend. There is no temptation to remain within
the city; the streets are little better than open
sewers, and the rivers, which should be its glory
and ornament, are left to roam at large, and to
pollute where they should purify. But the situation
of Damascus is unrivalled. The rich valley, which
tradition claims as the Garden of Eden, lies at the
base of the Antilibanon, and viewed from the
heights to the west, nothing can surpass the richness and beauty of its vegetation. The rich, spark-

ling waters of the " Abana and Pharpar, better than all the waters of Israel," flow through and around the city, and nothing is wanted to make it the "garden of the world " but a little taste and industry, and the fostering care of a paternal government. The blight of the Moslem is more conspicuous here than in any part of Palestine, because perhaps the gifts and beauties of nature are more apparent.

Through the kindness of Mr. Rogers, I was permitted to visit two or three of the houses of the wealthy Greek residents. These were rich and gaudy in gilt and colouring. The buildings were in the form of a quadrangle, with a broad marble-paved court, and marble fountains in the centre, reminding one in some respects of the splendid Moorish buildings in Seville and other cities in Spain, but sadly deficient in the exquisite taste that distinguished the Moors of that country.

My last afternoon was spent in the schools. Of all the cities in the East, there is none that may be said to have such a claim on our help and sympathy as Damascus. It was the first Christian city in the world, and is now only waiting for the husbandman. Both Greek and Jew are sending their children to Protestant schools, and only means and teachers are wanted to satisfy the demand for instruction. Mrs. Thompson's school was established after the massacre of 1860, and her religious and benevolent purpose is too well known to require any eulogium from me; but it is impossible to look into the faces of those neat, intelligent, and now happy-looking children, the survivors of those sad events, without deep sympathy, and prayers that a blessing may attend the labours of this excellent and benevolent lady and her coadjutors.

The weather had now become fine, and appeared to be settled, and I decided to join two gentlemen who were about to proceed to Baalbek. They had engaged an intelligent Maronite, who was well acquainted with the route, and promised us accommodation without the necessity of tents and heavy equipage. We had therefore very little preparation to make, and only took an additional man to look after our horses. Before starting, we made arrangements with the French Diligence Company to reserve the coupé for us on a given day, on paying the full fare from Damascus, that we might join it *en route* on our return to Beyrout. We divided the journey into two days: the first was occupied in a very long ride to Surghâya; and starting the second day at daylight, we reached Baalbek at 11.30 A.M.

If the reader will glance at the map of Palestine, he will find that this city lies almost due north from Damascus, about forty-five miles, in a valley under the Antilibanon. The modern town lies a little to the east of the temples, and is a miserable Arab village of eighty to one hundred huts.

My chief object in visiting these stupendous ruins was that I might realise my early impressions of those beautiful pictures, with which I was familiar, when I had little hope of seeing the originals; and all my expectations were more than realised, and the impression they have left on my mind is altogether beyond description. The day was clear and beautiful, and we were able to inspect these magnificent ruins under the most favourable circumstances. The situation of this ancient city is not unlike that of Ephesus. The ruins lie partly in a valley at the base of Antilibanon. The walls of the city are about two and a half miles in circumference, only small portions of which are now standing. The whole space within these walls is strewed with ruins, consisting of broken columns, architraves, cornices, and portions of friezes, exquisitely sculptured, giving one some faint idea of the original beauty and magnitude of these buildings.

We found a French artist taking photographs of the various ruins, and supplied ourselves with copies. The first view of these temples is grand and imposing, and being constructed of close white limestone, they have all the appearance of marble, and are so massive that, like Ephesus, nothing but repeated earthquakes could have shattered these walls and porticos. The late David Roberts says: " It is difficult to convey, even with the pencil, any idea of the magnificence of these ruins, the beauty of their form, the exquisite richness of the ornaments, or the vast magnitude of their dimensions. One scroll alone of Acanthus leaves, with groups of children, and panthers intertwined, would form a great work of itself." The architecture is evidently of different ages. The huge masses of stone that form the substructures of platforms and walls, are of the Cyclopean period known as that of the Early Phœnician, and perhaps anterior to that of the Temple of Jerusalem; but the most beautiful of the ruins are of the Greek and Roman period. The limestone of which the platform and walls are formed was quarried in the neighbourhood, and some idea may be formed of the magnitude of the stones employed by referring to one which is now lying near the place from which it was quarried.

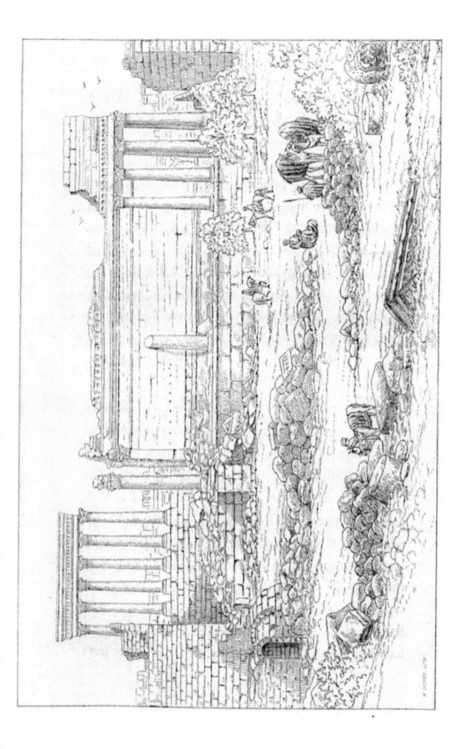

This stone measures about 70 feet long by 14 feet broad and 17 feet deep. The marvel is how stones of this size were moved and elevated to their present position in the buildings.

The ruins consist of three distinct buildings, viz., the two greater Temples, and the lesser one, called the Circular Temple. The Great Temple covers an area of nearly 1,000 feet from east to west, and about 500 feet from south to north. A few of the columns on the south side are still standing, with the foundations of the peristyle and the base of the columns. These stand on an elevated platform about 40 feet from the plain. This Temple seems to have consisted of a centre court of 400 feet square, surrounded with portico and peristyle, the columns of which were 65 feet high, and over this was an entablature of 14 feet, formed of immense blocks of stone beautifully and elaborately sculptured. The next and most magnificent of all the ruins has been called the Temple of the Sun. The walls, and some portions of the peristyle and portico, are still standing; these are raised on a platform of 30 feet from the ground. Six of the columns, with their architrave, are still in their original position. The building is in the form of the Parthenon of Athens, but larger, and of a different order, this being pure

P

Corinthian. The height of the columns now standing is about 65 feet, including capitals, with a diameter at the base of 7 feet, and resting on these are the remains of a beautiful architrave. In the west wall of this Temple are three stones which measure 61 feet each, and, as we said before, we marvel how, or by what machinery, they could have been raised to their present position. But the marvel of this building is the remains of the great portal. It is 21 feet wide and 42 feet high, surmounted by an architrave and frieze of nearly 20 feet. This magnificent portal was shattered by an earthquake in 1759. The centre stone of the lintel has given way, and now both sides hang in the air, but even in its ruins it forms one of the most wonderful works of skill and labour in the world. The great artist to whom reference has already been made says of this portal: "This is perhaps the most elaborate work, as well as the most exquisite in its detail, of anything of its kind in the world." The last and smallest of these ruins is called the Circular Temple, lying to the south-east of the Great Temple. This was at one time used by the Greek Christians as a church, but is now neglected. It is perhaps the purest and most classical of all these buildings, and of the best period of

Greek art, and is supposed to have been dedicated to Venus. The walls and beautiful entablature are now rent and dilapidated, and as nothing is done to sustain them, the whole may in a short time be nothing but an indistinguishable heap of ruins.

It is rather curious that we should know less of this once magnificent city than of any other in Palestine. It is not once mentioned in sacred history that I am aware of, and it is but slightly referred to by Greek and Roman writers. Its origin is probably of prehistoric date, and may have been contemporary with Heliopolis, of Egypt, the name given to this city by the Greeks. There is no doubt, however, that it was an early and important city of the Phœnicians, and retained its importance down through the Greek and Roman period, till the blight of the Moslem fell upon it.

We had scarcely four hours to ride over these ruins, and of course had no time to look into details, but the *tout ensemble* has left on my mind a dream of pleasure and satisfaction which I find it impossible to describe, but which I can never forget; and if I had had no other object in my journey, I should consider the privilege of visiting these splendid ruins, before barbarism and earthquakes have strewed them over the ground, an ample reward for all my troubles and fatigues.   Returning by the old quarries, about two miles distant, we passed a ruin called the Arab Temple, supposed to be the tomb of some Moslem saint.   The granite columns and architraves are evidently the remains of some former Greek or Roman temple.

A ride of four hours brought us back to Surghâya, to our previous night's quarters, a small upper room in the house of a Christian family, who made us as comfortable as their limited means would admit. At daybreak next morning we started again across country, through wadies and along the spurs of the mountains.   About noon, after a hard ride, we reached the halfway-house on the main road between Damascus and Beyrout, and had time for refreshments, and to settle with and discharge our useful and attentive dragoman and equipage, before the diligence came up.   We found the coupé reserved for us and took possession of it.   These three days of mental and bodily fatigue were almost too much for me.   The two young Frenchmen that accompanied me were very kind and attentive to me, and wrapped up in a corner of the coupé, the bracing air of the Lebanon "wooed nature's sweet restorer, balmy sleep," and I did not awake till we had nearly reached Beyrout, in the dusk of the evening.

Next morning I found there would be no steamer passing to the south for two days; at which I was not sorry, as it gave me some time to rest, to write up my journal, and to renew my acquaintance with the Rev. Dr. Bliss, President of the Syrian Protestant College; with Dr. Van Dyck, the great Arabic scholar, now engaged on a translation of the Bible into Arabic; and with the Rev. Dr. Thomson, author of "The Land and the Book." I was also able to spend the greater part of a day with Mr. and Mrs. Mentor Mott, the latter sister to Mrs. Thompson, to whose benevolent efforts I have already referred. Their school is one of the most healthy, cheering, and happy sights in Syria. They have from sixty to seventy girls in their charge, many of them the children of well-to-do Jews and Mohammedans, as well as Greek Christians. Attached is the Normal Training Institution, in which the pupil teachers receive a higher grade of education. Mr. Mott is now endeavouring to establish an ophthalmic hospital in connection with the mission. At present he is limited for means and space, but has already in his charge ten poor helpless children, some of them partially, and others

totally, blind, from this sad disease. A number of
benevolent ladies in England have formed a com-
mittee for the support of these " Anglo-Syrian
Female Schools," and I am persuaded that many
more would give their aid if they knew the bless-
ings, temporal and spiritual, that attend these
efforts, and could see the self-denying labours and
devotion of these missionaries. Here, as everywhere else, the Americans are in the van of missionary labours. They bring with them all the
energy, moral courage, and practical application of
their countrymen. It is not only what they do
themselves, but they have stirred up the dark and
dormant spirits of the Greek and Latin Churchmen,
who are now establishing opposition schools, and
giving their young of both sexes a much higher
standard of education. There are upwards of
seventy pupils in Dr. Bliss's Institution, receiving
instructions in Arabic, literature, mathematics, and
modern languages. Of this number, twenty are in
the medical department, under a professor and four
tutors, and all of them are more or less instructed
in Biblical literature.

My last day in Palestine happened to be on
Sunday, a quiet English or Scottish Sabbath. The
service from 10 to 11 A.M. was in Arabic, for

Jews, Syrians, and Greeks, and at eleven the English service commenced. It was Communion Sabbath, and there were assembled American Congregationalists, Scottish Presbyterians, and members of the Church of England, united in brotherly love and charity. It was a gratifying sight and a happy contrast to the rival sects of the so-called Christians whom I saw a few Sundays before in the Church of the Holy Sepulchre, and whose mutual jealousies, and often disgraceful antagonism, have brought such shame on the name of Christian. One must visit this land to see the contrast between the simple forms of our primitive church and the " vain repetitions," rites, and perversions of human invention. It cannot be seen at Rome, for there the scarlet conclave, like the kuife-grinders of Sheffield, admit of no opposition, and have at times carried out their "corporate rights and privileges " quite as severely as our misled countrymen. In this instance, at least, the Pope might take a lesson from the Sultan !

Altogether there is a healthy tone about this Beyrout, such as one rarely sees in the East; and if I were forced to reside in Palestine, I think I should prefer Beyrout to any city I have visited on this journey. There is a circle of cheerful social and educated men here that makes society very agreeable. The inhabitants number about 65,000, of whom 20,000 are Mohammedans, the remainder Christians of various denominations, and a few Jews. The situation of the town is also very pretty. The suburban villas and residences of the Europeans stretch along the promontory which forms the south of St. George's Bay, over fertile undulations, covered with mulberry, fig, palm, and cypress trees, and vineyards. Rising from its base, away to the north, is seen the snowy range of the Lebanon. It is, moreover, the only tolerable harbour along the whole of this coast. Many persons land here to take the journey through Palestine; but I think this is a mistake, as the travellers get into the difficulties of the journey before they are prepared for them. I would suggest proceeding direct to Jerusalem by Jaffa, and from thence making short excursions, such as I have described in previous chapters, which are attended with few difficulties, and prepare the tourist for more extended journeys.

Before quitting this land, I would offer a few parting words to such of my readers as may contemplate making this journey.

CHAPTER XVI.

WHEN I began to make preparations for the tour to Palestine, I had certain misgivings, as most persons will have who have read the many conflicting opinions of writers on this subject, and I wrote to a dear friend in Jerusalem to help me out with his advice and experience, and the reply was: "If you bring a fair amount of good health to rough it a little, and 'money in thy purse,' there are no difficulties or troubles in the journey you propose." I found this opinion correct to the letter.

I do not think it advisable for persons liable to illness from irregular diet, exposure, and sudden changes of temperature, to undertake this journey, except with great caution and in company of friends; but if this risk is provided for their pleasure will be the greater, and in the matter of money, the expense may be very much modified by a little judicious management. There are a number of dragomans of well-known experience who hang about the consulates, and whose chief aim seems to be

to throw difficulties in the way, and to magnify their
own services and importance. I was a little uneasy,
on reading a late volume by one of the most
talented and indefatigable travellers in Palestine,
when he spoke of "a pile of sovereigns on the table
of his consul, and nothing would satisfy the demands
of the dragoman." These men seem to know their
customers, and augment the difficulties and demands
accordingly. When we were about to start for the
Dead Sea and the Jordan for five or six days, we
told our sprightly and intelligent young dragoman,
Abraham, that we were prepared to make the
journey under his care, that we would leave our
luggage at Jerusalem, and the three of us would pay
him one pound each per day as long as we required
his services; this sum to cover all expenses, including
any guide or protection that might be necessary, to
which he cheerfully agreed. I have heard of three
times this sum being paid with less satisfaction than
we experienced. We talked of making a quick
journey to Petra and back to Jerusalem, and one of
these "experienced" dragomans told us he could not
undertake the journey, and pay all the demands of
Bedouin chiefs, under one hundred pounds each for
four persons. I learned that two artists had made
the journey from Jerusalem to Petra and back,

and brought a very valuable collection of photographs and drawings, and had accomplished their objects in safety at one-fourth this expense.

One other suggestion I would venture to offer to those who wish merely to take a glimpse of Palestine to assist their reading and study of sacred history, and who have not been accustomed to travel in distant lands or to depend on their own resources —viz., to put themselves in the hands of Mr. Henry Gaze or Mr. Cook, who have been so highly commended by all the travellers who have availed themselves of their services, and under whose guidance and experience they have been able to see more, at less trouble and expense, than is possible for any one making a rapid journey on their own account. They need not be daunted by the sneers of those who can afford to travel in the suite of princes, or have time and means to prolong their journey. They will find that many professional men of eminence have put themselves under the guidance of these gentlemen, and speak most highly of the advantages of their arrangements.

The reader will perhaps inquire how we got home? I shall sum up this information very briefly. I took a passage in the Russian steamer that passes Beyrout for Alexandria. We stopped a

few hours at Acre and Jaffa to land and take in
passengers and cargo, and on the second day arrived
at Port Said, named after the late Pacha of Egypt.
I was prepared for a surprise here; but the trans-
formation was altogether beyond conception. A
few years ago, this long stretch of sandy desert,
lying between the sea and the Lake Menzaleh, was a
desolate waste, without an inhabitant. There is now
a city of 8,000 Europeans and 3,000 Arabs; several
comfortable hotels, avenues laid out in streets, villas,
and gardens, literally raised on the sand. I called
on the British consul, a native of Malta, and surgeon
to the hospital. I found him an excellent botanist,
and a man of good taste and education. He has
managed to form a garden on the sand with a crust
of manure and artificial soil, in which he has a fine
collection of flowers and plants of both tropical and
temperate zones. This is only one of the many
pretty little oases that have been created in this
desert within the last five or six years. These
gardens are nourished by the rich and fertilising
water of the Nile, which is conducted in pipe conduits from the fresh water canal at Ismailia, and of
which I shall have occasion to speak hereafter.

The entrance to the harbour is protected by two
breakwaters, running out about two miles into the

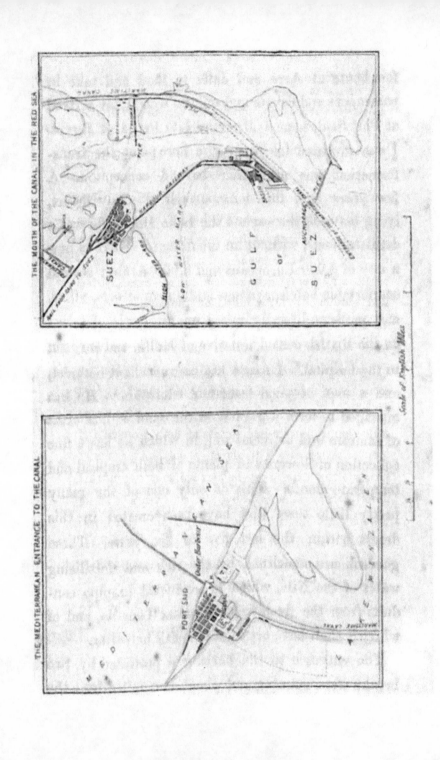

THE MOUTH OF THE CANAL IN THE RED SEA

THE MEDITERRANEAN ENTRANCE TO THE CANAL

Scale of English Miles

sea, to the south of the Gulf of Pelusus, and near
the eastern branch of the Nile. These breakwaters,
which are meant to keep back the great body of
sand which rolls in from the mouths of the Nile,
are formed of large blocks of artificial stones, such
as are used on the Dover pier, composed of concrete
and lime, weighing thirty tons, and at the cost of
about £14 each. The stones are run out, and
tumbled over without any regard to order, and may
ultimately be carried out a distance of four miles.
At the entrance to the lake a large dock, or basin,
has been formed, in which there were fifty or sixty
vessels lying, from 200 to 800 tons.

M. de Lesseps had just arrived from France the
day before, and had proceeded to Ismailia, and as I
was fortunate enough to have an introduction to
that gentleman from a fellow-passenger, I arranged
to leave the following morning at 7 A.M. in the
little steamer that runs daily to that station. Nothing could be more desolate, and, at the same
time, more wonderful and interesting, than this six
or seven hours' sail. The canal skirts the eastern
side of the Lake Menzaleh for about twenty-two
miles, then enters a short cutting of sand-hills into
the scattered and irregular Lake Ballah, where
there is again a long cutting of eight or ten miles,

to Lake Timseh, on the border of which is the new
town and port of Ismailia, called after the present
ruler of Egypt. This place is about equi-distant
from the Mediterranean and the Red Sea, fifty miles
distant from each. Here the fresh water canal,
proceeding from a branch of the Nile at Zagazig,
joins the great canal by a branch and lock, and
runs nearly parallel with it until it reaches Suez.
It is impossible to estimate sufficiently the immense
advantages of this fresh water canal to Egypt,
without which the thousands of workmen and
animals employed could not have been sustained.
Along its whole line have sprung up a succession
of richly-cultivated fields, on what was formerly a
barren burning plain.

I cannot better describe what this place was
before the magic wand of M. de Lesseps passed
over it, than by quoting a few lines of Daniel
Lange, Esq., the able and indefatigable English
director of the canal company, from a lecture given
by him before the Society of Arts :—

"How impressive," he says, "is that dreary
shadowless desert, with its breathless silence, its
awful solitude, and solemn repose! In this dreary
waste there is not an object to throw out a shadow
which would foretell the fall of evening. Centuries

have passed over this unchanging surface, and daily the same unvarying scene continues.

"It was in the midst of that dreary shadowless desert that a town had to be erected, and it was done. Ismailia now stands on the scene I have described, and the desert has been made to blossom like a rose."

The town of Ismailia is now studded with beautiful gardens of flowers, fruits, and vegetables, and from a great reservoir at this place, the healthy and fertilising water of the Nile is conveyed by pipes parallel with the sea canal as far as Port Said.

Had M. de Lesseps done nothing more for Egypt than conducting this stream of fresh water through the desert from sea to sea, he would have left a monument of his skill and perseverance far more glorious than any of the Pharaohs. On presenting my letter of introduction to M. de Lesseps I was received by him with that kindness and cordiality which characterises his manner to all, and particularly to his English visitors. There is a frank, open, and manly bearing about this gentleman that puts the stranger at once at ease with him. I cannot speak too highly of his attention and desire to afford me every information. I received at his office a number of maps, plans, and diagrams, and I find I have filled nearly twenty pages of my journal with descriptions, and the opinions I heard and formed of the works; but these have been so fully explained by Mr. Fowler, the eminent engineer, and other correspondents of the " Times," and by the admirable illustrations of Mr. Simpson, that I shall spare the reader these details, and simply refer to my own experience, and the information I gathered on the spot.

Perhaps it may be said that " we have had more than enough of the Suez Canal ;" but I venture to think that this great work, and the results likely to follow its entire completion, cannot be too often brought to public attention.

It would be impossible here to convey to any one who has not followed the history of this enterprise, the difficulties which the managers and engineers have had to encounter and overcome in their undertaking, apart from the discouragement they met with both in France and England.

There is still an impression on the minds of these gentlemen, which I would desire to remove, or at least to modify, that there was a political opposition on the part of the British Government to this undertaking. I have every reason to believe that the personal opposition and discouragement of

the late Lord Palmerston, was less a political question than a financial caution to individuals " to look
to their pockets, and not to be carried away by
sanguine men who had nothing to lose and everything to gain by a protracted investment of capital
in the sands of Egypt." I confess, with some degree of shame, that I was one of those who had little
hope of seeing M. de Lesseps' plans and expectations
realised. As far as the execution of the work is
concerned, these doubts and misgivings have all
been dispelled; but it yet remains to be proved
whether we are right or wrong as to the financial
results.

It is a curious coincidence, and worthy of notice,
that the two great contemporary dramatic authors,
Shakespeare and Marlowe, should have prefigured
the two great events of the present century.

In "Midsummer Night's Dream" Puck says :

> " I'll put a girdle round about the earth
> In forty minutes."

And the hero of Marlowe's tragedy of " Tambur-
laine the Great " says :

> " And here, not far from Alexandria, where the
> Terrene (Mediterranean) and the Red Sea meet,
> Being distant less than one hundred leagues,
> I mean to cut a channel to them both,
> That men might quickly sail to India," etc., etc.

Q

Marlowe may have heard of the Pharaoh Canal; but this was simply a fresh water passage from the Nile to the Red Sea, and only suited for small boats.

It is instructive to contrast the history and execution of these two works. Herodotus informs us that the ancient canal was commenced about seven hundred years before our era. " That it was 100 miles long, and about nine feet deep, and occupied one hundred years in its construction, and that 120,000 Egyptians, or slaves, perished in the labour." M. de Lesseps' great work was carried through in ten years, with no greater mortality than would have occurred in the ordinary course of labour.

The length of the canal, running nearly north and south, is 100 miles, and the depth of water is supposed to be 26 feet. The width between the banks varies from 200 to 300 feet; where the slopes are great, it is as much as 340 feet; and it is about 72 feet at the bottom.

The whole of these works, where water is available, have been excavated by the aid of three descriptions of machines—first, the common dredge; this deposits the earth in punts, which are conveyed to another powerful machine called the elevator, which raises these punts and runs them out over the bank; and a third called the receiver, having a long semicircular tube, carries the deposit, by the aid of a water pump, some sixty, or seventy feet over the banks. Several of these machines were at work as we passed up, deepening the canal, and we were struck with their power and magnitude, and were told that the larger ones cost as much as £40,000 each.

At this time, the maritime canal was open for navigation only as far as Ismailia; there we took the railway at 5 P.M., and we arrived at Suez at 9 P.M. Next morning early, we visited the great dock and works that are going forward at the anchorage four miles below Suez. Here a large portion of land is being reclaimed from the shallow waters of the gulf, and docks and warehouses are being erected, to which the railway will run, in direct communication with Alexandria. This will be a great saving of time, trouble, and expense, as the passengers and cargo are now conveyed from the large steamers in small boats over the shallows to Suez. It will also form the Suez harbour, communicating with the canal, which, entering the Red Sea at the eastern point of the gulf, is carried by a deep cutting through the shallow lagoon to the anchorage and docks, about two and a-half miles to the south of Suez.

Immediately after breakfast, a small party of us procured horses and rode partly along the works of the maritime canal to Chalouf, about fourteen miles from the entrance of the canal into the Red Sea. These fourteen miles have been the most difficult portion of the undertaking, as the line has been crossed by strata of rock, the removal of which has been attended with great labour and delay. The opinions at present on the commercial success of this undertaking are very conflicting. The expense of keeping the canal open will no doubt absorb a large amount of the receipts, whatever they may be, but it is quite impossible as yet to form any opinion as to the extent to which shippers will avail themselves of this mode of transit. (See Appendix.) Whatever may be the commercial results, there can be but one feeling, that of respect and admiration, for the man who planned and carried out this undertaking with such indomitable pluck and perseverance, in the face of every obstacle and opposition. All honour, then, to the Chevalier M. de Lesseps.

Before leaving Suez it may be interesting to contrast its present prosperity with the former miserable condition of this place.

It is just thirty years since I first visited this port, on my way to India, when the "overland journey" was something to talk about. We were four days on the Mahmoudieh Canal and the Nile; when it was sometimes a question with us whether we were to be broiled in the sun, or eaten alive by the vermin collected in the boat. Great preparations had to be made at Cairo, with Bedouins and camels, and we were part of three days in crossing the desert to Suez, in the rear of some 300 Moslem fanatics making their way to Mecca. Suez then consisted of a miserable Arab village of 1,000 inhabitants, with a dilapidated khan for pilgrims. Our Moslem companions and their cattle occupied the courtyard and ground-floor, and our party of five were lodged in an empty upper room. We were detained here four days waiting for the little steamer that ran once a month between Suez and Bombay. Our small water supply was brought across the desert, hot and tasteless, and our food was eggs and starved chickens. Now the fresh water of the Nile is brought to the door, there are half-a-dozen comfortable restaurants and the splendid Peninsular and Oriental Hotel, where kings and princes are accommodated with luxury, a large staff of official and commercial Europeans, and a town of 8,000 inhabitants.

The line of railway has been changed lately, and instead of going direct by Cairo, takes a more northward route, and has a short branch to the canal port of Ismailia, then strikes westward across the Nile. There is a branch to Cairo, but the direct line is to Alexandria. We left Suez at 8 A.M. and reached Alexandria at 8 P.M. A considerable portion of the line skirts the fresh water canal, and here again we see the marvellous and incalculable benefits conferred on this desert tract by irrigation. While on this subject my thoughts turn naturally to India. True, this spot is but a miniature of space and necessities compared to our vast possessions in India, but with such fertilising rivers as the Jumna and Ganges, something more might be done to stay the periodical famines in Upper India, such as I witnessed in 1837. It is only a matter of money and labour to save the lives of millions, and I have often heard it remarked that the money spent on that unprovoked and most calamitous war of Afghanistan would have irrigated the whole of Upper India.

On my arrival at Alexandria I found five steamers about to start, viz., the Peninsular and Oriental Company's steamer, the Russian boat in which

I came to Port Said, the Austrian Lloyds for Trieste, the French Messagerie for Marseilles, and the Italian boat for Brindisi. My intention was to have taken the latter, *and* to have come home through Italy; but I was still suffering from the effects of my Palestine journey, and was not inclined to trust myself to the conceit and indifference of Italian railway *employés* and physicians. So I took my passage in the old Ripon, where I found a kind and skilful friend in the surgeon, and with the agreeable society of old Indians, and the calm and delightful freshness of the Mediterranean, I was soon set up again and restored to health and appetite. There were few incidents on the voyage. On the fifth day we passed Sicily and the Straits of Messina; and on the sixth day we entered the beautiful and picturesque scenery of the Straits of Bonifacio, and sailed close under Caprera, where we ran up the union jack, and were answered by the Italian flag. Garibaldi and two friends came out of his cottage and returned our salute. The general is a great favourite with the folks on board the Ripon. He went with them to England, and endeared himself to all on board by that frank, gentle, and fascinating manner which wins on every one who has the privilege of his society.

On the seventh day from Alexandria we arrived at Marseilles, and in thirty-six hours were in London, after three months' journey, the most interesting and instructive that it has been my fortune to enjoy.

APPENDIX.

SINCE the writer's return from Egypt, the successful opening of the Suez Canal is an accomplished fact, and our most earnest wishes and hopes have been in a great degree realised, and many of our doubts dispelled.

There are still difficulties to be overcome, and it will require from one to two million pounds of additional capital to render the navigation safe and expeditious.

The two great breakwaters on the Mediterranean must be carried farther out, made more solid, and have lighthouses erected on their extreme points. Some of the abrupt bends in the south portion of the Canal must be cut down, so that vessels of great length may pass through without injury to their screws by coming in contact with the banks.

If these alterations and improvements cannot be

R

effected by private capital, it will be the duty of the governments of Europe to come forward with the necessary aid and encouragement to complete the work; and I would venture to suggest that there is no nation under such great obligations as England and its dependencies to aid and maintain this great international enterprise, which has brought her most important colonies to within half their former distance.

The following table will show to what extent the English shippers have already availed themselves of this *short cut to the East.* In the month of May last there passed through the Canal—

27 English vessels,	measuring		28,000	tons.
8 French	,,	,,	7,500	,,
3 Italian	,,	,,	1,400	,,
1 Turkish	,,	,,	1,100	,,
1 Austrian	,,	,,	730	,,

It will thus be seen that the English tonnage passing through the Canal was more than double that of all the other nations put together.

The greatest triumph of the month we quote was the passage of the English Government transport steamer "Jumna," of 4,000 tons, with H.M.'s 77th Regiment, and other passengers, in perfect safety.

Two or three smaller vessels have met with some detention, and slight injury to their screws, probably from getting out of the channel; but these are casualties which some additional expense and labour will overcome.

I may conclude these remarks by a quotation from the able address of Daniel A. Lange, Esq., read before the Society of Arts, to which I have already referred :—

"Villages will soon usurp the place of solitary dwellings, and these again grow into populous towns; and a blank, dismal waste shall be changed into a scene fruitful with life and hope, sown on the barren sands of Egypt.

"Surely this is a work worthy the ambition of men! Of these, at least, it cannot be said :—' *Eheu! vitam perdidi operose nihil agendo*' (Alas! I have wasted my days in toil and have done nothing). It is impossible to predict the advantages which may accrue from opening a maritime highway between the two hemispheres, bringing into closer union a population of 300 millions in the western and 600 millions of souls in the eastern quarter of the globe. Can this commingling of races fail to be the means of opening a path for the introduction of that light which it is the missionary's joy to spread in distant lands, brilliant with the glare of solar rays, but o'ershadowed by the darkness of unbelief? Is it not meeting him half-way in his holy work, and preparing a stupendous revolution in the traffic of the world, by changing the geographical proximity of England's great possessions in the East?"

LONDON: R. K. BURT AND CO., PRINTERS, WINE OFFICE COURT, E.C.

CPSIA information can be obtained
at www.ICGtesting.com
Printed in the USA
BVHW070207080921
616221BV00002B/372

9 783348 061056